CAMBRIDGE LIBRARY COLLECTION

Books of enduring scholarly value

English Men of Letters

In the 1870s, Macmillan publishers began to issue a series of books called
'English Men of Letters' – biographies of English writers by other English
writers. The general editor of the series was the journalist, critic, politician,
and supporter (and later biographer) of Gladstone, John Morley (1838–
1923). The first volume published was Samuel Johnson, by Leslie Stephen
(1878), and the first series (which continued until 1892) eventually consisted
of 39 volumes. The aim was to provide a short introduction to each subject
and his works, but also that the life should illuminate the works, and vice
versa. All the subjects were men, as were all but one of the authors (Mrs
Oliphant on Sheridan); and all but one (Hawthorne) were English or Irish.
The subjects range chronologically from Chaucer to Thackeray and Dickens,
and an important feature of the series is that many of the authors (Henry
James on Hawthorne, Ward on Dickens) were discussing writers of the
previous generation, and some (Trollope on Thackeray) had even known
their subjects personally. The series exemplifies the British approach to
literary biography and criticism at the end of the nineteenth century, and also
reveals which authors were at that time regarded as canonical.

Charles Lamb

Written by clergyman Alfred Ainger (1837–1904), this 1882 biography of
writer Charles Lamb (1775–1834) is the twenty-first book in the first series
of 'English Men of Letters'. Charles Lamb began publishing his poetry in the
late 1790s. Both he and his sister Mary (1764–1847), who had been released
into Charles' care after killing their mother in a fit of insanity in 1796, began
writing for children with the encouragement of William Godwin, their works
including the *Tales from Shakespeare* (1807) for which they are best known.
Lamb was also widely regarded for his skill as an essayist, and particularly
for his *Essays of Elia*. Ainger devoted much of his career to Lamb's life and
writings, including a six-volume edited collection of Lamb's work. His
biography focuses on Lamb's literary output and his place as a critic as well as
the events of the writer's life.

T0382638

Cambridge University Press has long been a pioneer in the reissuing of out-of-print titles from its own backlist, producing digital reprints of books that are still sought after by scholars and students but could not be reprinted economically using traditional technology. The Cambridge Library Collection extends this activity to a wider range of books which are still of importance to researchers and professionals, either for the source material they contain, or as landmarks in the history of their academic discipline.

Drawing from the world-renowned collections in the Cambridge University Library, and guided by the advice of experts in each subject area, Cambridge University Press is using state-of-the-art scanning machines in its own Printing House to capture the content of each book selected for inclusion. The files are processed to give a consistently clear, crisp image, and the books finished to the high quality standard for which the Press is recognised around the world. The latest print-on-demand technology ensures that the books will remain available indefinitely, and that orders for single or multiple copies can quickly be supplied.

The Cambridge Library Collection will bring back to life books of enduring scholarly value (including out-of-copyright works originally issued by other publishers) across a wide range of disciplines in the humanities and social sciences and in science and technology.

Charles Lamb

ALFRED AINGER

CAMBRIDGE
UNIVERSITY PRESS

CAMBRIDGE UNIVERSITY PRESS

Cambridge, New York, Melbourne, Madrid, Cape Town,
Singapore, São Paolo, Delhi, Tokyo, Mexico City

Published in the United States of America by Cambridge University Press, New York

www.cambridge.org
Information on this title: www.cambridge.org/9781108034586

© in this compilation Cambridge University Press 2011

This edition first published 1882
This digitally printed version 2011

ISBN 978-1-108-03458-6 Paperback

English Men of Letters

EDITED BY JOHN MORLEY

CHARLES LAMB

CHARLES LAMB

BY

ALFRED AINGER

London:

MACMILLAN AND CO.

1882.

PREFATORY NOTE.

THE writings of Charles Lamb abound in biographical matter. To them, and to the well-known volumes of the late Mr. Justice Talfourd, I am mainly indebted for the material of which this memoir is composed.

I have added a complete list of the chief works from which information about Lamb and his sister has been obtained. I have also had the advantage of communication with those who were personally acquainted with Lamb, and have received from others valuable assistance in exploring less known sources of information.

Among those to whom my acknowledgments for much kindness are due, I would mention Mrs. Arthur Tween, a daughter of that old and loyal friend of the Lamb family, Mr. Randal Norris; Mr. James Crossley, of Manchester; Mr. Edward FitzGerald; Mr. W Aldis Wright; and last, not least, my friend Mr. J. E. Davis, of the Middle Temple, whose kind interest in this little book has been unfailing.

A. A.

HAMPSTEAD,
December, 1881.

AUTHORITIES CONSULTED.

1. The Essays of Elia, and other writings, in prose and verse, of Charles Lamb.
2. Letters of Charles Lamb, with a Sketch of his Life by Thomas Noon Talfourd 1837
3. Final Memorials of Charles Lamb, &c., by Thomas Noon Talfourd 1848
4. Charles Lamb: A Memoir, by Barry Cornwall . . 1866
5. Charles and Mary Lamb: Poems, Letters, and Remains, by W. Carew Hazlitt 1874
6. Gillman's Life of Coleridge, vol. i. . . . 1838
7. Cottle's Early Recollections of Coleridge . . . 1837
8. Alsop's Letters, Conversations, and Recollections of Coleridge 1836
9. My Friends and Acquaintance, by P. G. Patmore . 1854
10. Autobiography of Leigh Hunt 1850
11. Memoirs of William Hazlitt, by W. Carew Hazlitt . 1867
12. Literary Reminiscences, by Thomas Hood (in *Hood's Own*) 1839
13. Haydon's Autobiography and Journals . . 1853
14. Diary of Henry Crabb Robinson 1869
15. Memoir of Charles Mathews (the elder), by Mrs. Mathews 1838
16. Life and Correspondence of Robert Southey . . 1849
17. Obituary Notices, Reminiscences, Essays, &c., in various magazines and reviews.

CONTENTS.

a

x   CONTENTS.

CHARLES LAMB

CHARLES LAMB.

CHAPTER I.

BOYHOOD—THE TEMPLE AND CHRIST'S HOSPITAL.

(1775—1789.)

" I was born and passed the first seven years of my life
in the Temple. Its church, its halls, its gardens, its
fountain, its river, I had almost said—for in those young
years what was this king of rivers to me but a stream
that watered our pleasant places ?—these are of my oldest
recollections." In this manner does Charles Lamb, in an
essay that is one of the masterpieces of English prose,
open for us those passages of autobiography which happily
abound in his writings. The words do more than fix
places and dates. They strike the key in which his early
life was set—and the later life, hardly less. The genius
of Lamb was surely guided into its special channel by the
chance that the first fourteen years of his life were passed,
as has been said, " between cloister and cloister," between
the mediæval atmosphere of the quiet Temple and that of
the busy school of Edward VI.

Charles Lamb was born on the 10th of February, 1775
in Crown Office Row in the Temple, the line of buildings

facing the garden and the river he has so lovingly com-
memorated.   His father, John Lamb, who had come up
a country boy from Lincolnshire to seek his fortune in
the great city, was clerk and servant to Mr. Samuel Salt,
a Bencher of the Inner Temple.   He had married Elizabeth Field, whose mother was for more than fifty years
housekeeper at the old mansion of the Plumers, Blakesware in Hertfordshire, the Blakesmoor of the *Essays
of Elia*.   The issue of this marriage was a family of
seven children, only three of whom seem to have survived
their early childhood.   The registers of the Temple
Church record the baptisms of all the seven children,
ranging from the year 1762 to 1775.   Of the three who
lived, Charles was the youngest.   The other two were his
brother John, who was twelve years, and his sister Mary
Anne (better known to us as Mary), who was ten years
his senior.   The marked difference in age between Charles
and his brother and sister, must never be overlooked in
the estimate of the difficulties, and of the heroism, of his
later life.

In the essay already cited—that on the *Old Benchers
of the Inner Temple*—Charles has drawn for us a touching
portrait of his father, the barrister's clerk, under the name
of Lovel.   After speaking of Samuel Salt, the Bencher,
and certain indolent and careless ways from which he
" might have suffered severely if he had not had honest
people about him," he digresses characteristically into a
description of the faithful servant who was at hand to
protect him :—

Lovel took care of everything.   He was at once his clerk, his
good servant, his dresser, his friend, his " flapper," his guide, stop-
watch, auditor, treasurer.   He did nothing without consulting
Lovel, or failed in anything without expecting and fearing his

admonishing. He put himself almost too much in his hands,
had they not been the purest in the world. He resigned his
title almost to respect as a master, if Lovel could ever have
forgotten for a moment that he was a servant.

I knew this Lovel. He was a man of an incorrigible and
losing honesty. A good fellow withal, and "would strike." In
the cause of the oppressed he never considered inequalities, or
calculated the number of his opponents. He once wrested a
sword out of the hand of a man of quality that had drawn
upon him, and pommelled him severely with the hilt of it. The
swordsman had offered insult to a female—an occasion upon
which no odds against him could have prevented the interference
of Lovel. He would stand next day bare-headed to the same
person, modestly to excuse his interference, for Lovel never forgot rank, where something better was not concerned. Lovel
was the liveliest little fellow breathing ; had a face as gay as
Garrick's, whom he was said greatly to resemble (I have a portrait of him which confirms it) ; possessed a fine turn for
humorous poetry—next to Swift and Prior ; moulded heads in
clay or plaster of Paris to admiration, by the dint of natural
genius merely ; turned cribbage-boards, and such small cabinet
toys, to perfection ; took a hand at quadrille or bowls with equal
facility ; made punch better than any man of his degree in
England ; had the merriest quips and conceits, and was altogether as brimful of rogueries and inventions as you could
desire. He was a brother of the angle, moreover, and just such
a free, hearty, honest companion as Mr. Izaak Walton would
have chosen to go a-fishing with.

I saw him in his old age, and the decay of his faculties, palsy-
smitten, in the last sad stage of human weakness—" a remnant
most forlorn of what he was "—yet even then his eye would
light up upon the mention of his favourite Garrick. He was
greatest, he would say, in Bayes—" was upon the stage nearly
throughout the whole performance, and as busy as a bee." At
intervals, too, he would speak of his former life, and how he
came up a little boy from Lincoln to go to service, and how his
mother cried at parting with him, and how he returned after

some few years' absence in his smart new livery, to see her, and
she blessed herself at the change and could hardly be brought to
believe that it was " her own bairn." And then, the excitement
subsiding, he would weep, till I have wished that sad second-
childhood might have a mother still to lay its head upon her
lap. But the common mother of us all in no long time after
received him gently into hers.

I have digressed, in my turn, from the story of Charles
Lamb's own life, but it is not without interest to learn
from whom Charles inherited, not only something of his
versatility of gift, but his chivalry and tenderness.

The household in Crown Office Row were from the
beginning poor—of that we may feel certain. An aunt
of Charles, his father's sister, formed one of the family,
and contributed something to the common income, but
John Lamb the elder was the only other bread-winner.
And a barrister's clerk with seven children born to him
in a dozen years, even if lodging were found him, could
not have had much either to save or to spend. Before
seven years of age Charles got the rudiments of education
from a Mr. William Bird, whose schoolroom looked "into
a discoloured dingy garden in the passage leading from
Fetter Lane into Bartlett's Buildings." We owe this,
and some other curious information about the academy, to
a letter of Lamb's addressed in 1826 to Hone, the editor
of the *Every Day Book*. In that periodical had appeared
an account of a certain Captain Starkey, who was for
some time an assistant of Bird's. The mention of his old
teacher's name in this connexion called up in Lamb
many recollections of his earliest school-days, and produced the letter just named, full of characteristic matter.
The school, out of Fetter Lane, was a day-school for boys,
and an evening school for girls, and Charles and Mary had

the advantages, whatever they may have been, of its instruction. Starkey had spoken of Bird as "an eminent
writer, and teacher of languages and mathematics," &c.;
upon which Lamb's comment is, "Heaven knows what
languages were taught in it then! I am sure that neither
my sister nor myself brought any out of it but a little of
our native English." Then follow some graphic descriptions of the birch and the ferule, as wielded by Mr. Bird,
and other incidents of school-life :—

Oh, how I remember our legs wedged into those uncomfortable sloping desks, where we sat elbowing each other; and the
injunctions to attain a free hand, unattainable in that position;
the first copy I wrote after, with its moral lesson, "Art improves
nature;" the still earlier pot-hooks and the hangers, some
traces of which I fear may yet be apparent in this manuscript.

When Charles had absorbed such elementary learning
as was to be acquired under Mr. Bird and his assistants,
his father might have been much perplexed where to find
an education for his younger son, within his slender
means, and yet satisfying his natural ambition, had not a
governor of Christ's Hospital, of the name of Yeates, probably a friend of Samuel Salt, offered him a presentation to
that admirable charity. And on the 9th of October, 1782,
Charles Lamb, then in his eighth year, entered the institution, and remained there for the next seven years.

There is scarcely any portion of his life about which
Lamb has not himself taken his readers into his confidence,
and in his essay on *Witches and other Night-fears* he
has referred to his own sensitive and superstitious childhood, made more sensitive by the books, meat too strong
for childish digestion, to which he had free access in his
father's collection. "I was dreadfully alive to nervous

terrors. The night-time solitude and the dark were my
hell. The sufferings I endured in this nature would
justify the expression. I never laid my head on my
pillow, I suppose, from the fourth to the seventh or eighth
year of my life—so far as memory serves in things so long
ago—without an assurance, which realized its own pro-
phecy, of seeing some frightful spectre." Lamb was fond
both of exaggeration and of mystification, as we shall see
further on, but this account of his childhood is not incon-
sistent with descriptions of it from other sources. There
was a strain of mental excitability in all the family, and
in the case of Charles the nervousness of childhood was
increased by the impediment in his speech which remained
with him for life, and made so curious a part of his unique
personality. "He was an amiable, gentle boy," wrote
one who had been at school with him, "very sensible and
keenly observing, indulged by his school-fellows and by
his master on account of his infirmity of speech. I never
heard his name mentioned," adds this same school-fellow,
Charles Valentine Le Grice, "without the addition of
Charles, although, as there was no other boy of the name
of Lamb, the addition was unnecessary; but there was an
implied kindness in it, and it was a proof that his gentle
manners excited that kindness." Let us note here that
this term " gentle " (the special epithet of Shakspeare)
seems to have occurred naturally to all Lamb's friends, as
that which best described him. Coleridge, Wordsworth,
Landor, and Cary, recall no trait more tenderly than this.
And let us note also that the addition of his Christian
name (Lamb loved the use of it: "So Christians," he
said, "should call one another") followed him through
life and beyond it. There is perhaps no other English
writer who is so seldom mentioned by his surname alone.

Of Lamb's experience of school-life we are fortunate in having a full description in his essay, entitled *Recollections of Christ's Hospital*, published in 1818, and the sequel to it, called *Christ's Hospital five-and-thirty years ago* (one of the *Elia* essays), published two years later. But it requires some familiarity with Lamb's love of masquerading, already referred to, to disengage fact from fancy, and extract what refers to himself only, in these two papers. The former is, what it purports to be, a serious tribute of praise to the dignified and elevating character of the great Charity by which he had been fostered. It speaks chiefly of the young scholar's pride in the antiquity of the foundation and the monastic customs and ritual which had survived into modern times; of the Founder, "that godly and royal child, King Edward VI., the flower of the Tudor name—the young flower that was untimely cropped, as it began to fill our land with its early odours—the boy-patron of boys—the serious and holy child who walked with Cranmer and Ridley," with many touching reminiscences of the happy days spent in country excursions or visits to the sights of London. But in calling up these recollections it seems to have struck Lamb that his old school, like other institutions, had more than one side, and that the grievances of schoolboys, real and imaginary, as well as the humorous side of some of the regulations and traditions of the school, might supply material for another picture not less interesting. Accordingly, under the disguise of the signature *Elia*, he wrote a second account of his school, purporting to be a corrective of the over-colouring employed by "Mr. Lamb" in the former account. The writer affects to be a second witness called in to supplement the evidence of the first. "I remember L. at school," writes Lamb, under the signature of *Elia*.

"It happens very oddly that my own standing at Christ's
was nearly corresponding to his ; and with all gratitude
to him for his enthusiasm for the cloisters, I think he has
contrived to bring together whatever can be said in praise
of them, dropping all the other side of the argument most
ingeniously." This other side Lamb proceeds, with charming humour, to set forth, and he does so in the character
of one, a " poor friendless boy," whose parents were far
away at "sweet Calne, in Wiltshire," after which his heart
was ever yearning. The friendless boy whose personality
is thus assumed, was young Samuel Taylor Coleridge, who
had entered the school the same year as Lamb, though
three years his senior. Coleridge and Lamb were school-
fellows for the whole seven years of the latter's residence,
and from this early association arose a friendship as
memorable as any in English Literature. "Sweet Calne,
in Wiltshire," was thus one of Lamb's innocent mystifications. It was to the old home at "sweet Ottery St. Mary,"
in Devonshire, that young Samuel Taylor's thoughts
turned, when he took his lonely country rambles, or
shivered at the cold windows of the print-shops to while
away a winter's holiday.

In the character of Coleridge—though even here the
dramatic position is not strictly sustained—Lamb goes on
to relate, in the third person, many incidents of his own
boyish life, which differed of necessity from his friend's.
Charles Lamb was not troubled how to get through a
winter's day, for he had shelter and friendly faces within
easy reach of the school. "He had the privilege of going
to see them, almost as often as he wished, through some
invidious distinction which was denied to us. The present worthy sub-treasurer to the Inner Temple can ex-
plain how that happened. He had his tea and hot rolls

in the morning, while we were battening upon our quarter of a penny-loaf moistened with attenuated small-beer, in wooden piggins, smacking of the pitched leathern jack it was poured from." And the writer proceeds to draw a charming picture of some emissary from Lamb's home, his "maid or aunt," bringing him some home-cooked dainty, and squatting down on "some odd stone in a by-nook of the cloisters," while he partook of it. It suggests a pleasant and happy side to this portion of Charles Lamb's life. Humble as his home was, still home was near, and not unmindful of him; and even taking into account the severities of the discipline and other of the schoolboy's natural grievances, it would seem as if Lamb's school-years had a genial influence on his mind and spirit.

As to the education, in the common acceptation of the word, which he gained during those seven years at Christ's Hospital, we may form a very just notion. When he left the school, in his fifteenth year, in November, 1789, he was (according to his own statement made in more than one passage of his writings) deputy Grecian. Leigh Hunt, who entered the school two years after Lamb quitted it, and knew him intimately in later life, says the same thing. Talfourd seems to have applied to the school authorities for precise information, and gives a some-what different account. He says that " in the language of the school" he was "in Greek form, but not deputy Grecian." No such distinction is understood by " Blues " of a later date, but it may possibly mean that Lamb was doing deputy Grecians' work, though he was in some way technically disqualified from taking rank with them. " He had read," Talfourd goes on to tell us, " Virgil, Sallust, Terence, Lucian, and Xenophon, and had evinced

considerable skill in the niceties of Latin composition."
Latin, not Greek, was certainly his strong point, and with
Terence especially he shows a familiar acquaintance. He
wrote colloquial Latin with great readiness, and in turning
nursery rhymes into that language, as well as in one or
two more serious attempts, there are proofs of an ease of
expression very creditable to the scholarship of a boy of
fourteen.   And if (as appears certain) Lamb, though not
in the highest form at Christ's Hospital, had the benefit
of the teaching of the head-master, the Rev. James Boyer,
we have good reason for knowing that, pedant and tyrant
though Boyer may have been, he was no bad trainer for
such endowments as Coleridge's and Lamb's.

   Coleridge, in his *Biographia Literaria,* has drawn a
companion picture of the better side of Christ's Hospital
discipline, which may judiciously be compared with
Lamb's. "At school I enjoyed the inestimable advantage
of a very sensible, though at the same time, a very severe
master. He early moulded my taste to the preference of
Demosthenes to Cicero, of Homer and Theocritus to
Virgil, and again of Virgil to Ovid. He habituated me
to compare Lucretius (in such extracts as I then read),
Terence, and above all, the chaster poems of Catullus, not
only with the Roman poets of the so-called silver and
brazen ages, but with even those of the Augustan era ;
and on grounds of plain sense and universal logic, to see
and assert the superiority of the former, in the truth and
nativeness both of their thoughts and diction. At the
same time that we were studying the Greek tragic poets,
he made us read Shakespeare and Milton as lessons ; and
they were the lessons, too, which required most time and
trouble to *bring up,* so as to escape his censure. I learnt
from him that poetry, even that of the loftiest, and seem-

ingly that of the wildest odes, had a logic of its own as
severe as that of science, and more difficult, because more
subtle, more complex, and dependent on more and more
fugitive causes. In the truly great poets, he would say,
there is a reason assignable, not only for every word, but
for the position of every word ; and I well remember that,
availing himself of the synonymes to the Homer of Didy-
mus, he made us attempt to show, with regard to each,
why it would not have answered the same purpose,
and wherein consisted the peculiar fitness of the word in
the original text." Such a teacher, according to Coleridge,
was the guiding spirit of Christ's Hospital ; and even
allowing for Coleridge having in later life looked back
with magnifying eyes upon those early lessons, and *read
into* Boyer's teaching something that belonged rather to
the learner than the teacher, we need not doubt how
great were the young student's obligations to his master.
Lamb, who was three years younger, and never reached
the same position in the school, may not have benefited
directly by this method of Boyer's, but he was the
intimate companion of the elder schoolboy, and whatever
Boyer taught we may be sure was handed on in some
form or other to Lamb, tinged though it may have been
by the wondrous individuality of his friend.

For the influence of Coleridge over Lamb, during these
school-days and afterwards, is one of the most important
elements a biographer of Lamb has to take account of.
The boy, Samuel Taylor, had entered the school, as we
have seen, in the same year. He was a lonely, dreamy
lad, not living wholly apart from the pastimes of his
companions, wandering with them into the country, and
bathing in the New River, on the holidays of summer,
but taking his pleasure on the whole sadly, loving above

all things knowledge, and greedily devouring whatever
of that kind came in his way. Middleton, afterwards
Bishop of Calcutta, at the time a Grecian in the school,
found him one day reading Virgil in his play-hour, for his
own amusement, and reported the circumstance to Boyer,
who acted upon it by fostering henceforth in every way
his pupil's talent. A stranger who met the boy one day
in the London streets, lost in some day-dream, and moving
his arms as one who "spreadeth forth his hands to swim,"
extracted from him the confession that he was only thinking of Leander and the Hellespont. The stranger, impressed with the boy's love of books, subscribed for him
to a library in the neighbourhood of the school, and
young Coleridge proceeded, as he has told us, to read
"*through* the catalogue, folios and all, whether I understood them or did not understand them, running all risks
in skulking out to get the two volumes which I was entitled to have daily." With a full consciousness, as is
apparent, of his power, he seems at this age to have had
no desire for distinction, but only for enlarged experience.
At one time he wanted to be apprenticed to a shoemaker,
whose wife had shown him some kindness. At a later
time, encouraged by the example of his elder brother who
had come up to walk the London Hospital, he conceived
a passion for the medical profession and read every book
on doctoring he could lay his hands on. He went
through a phase of atheism—again, probably, out of sheer
curiosity—until he was judiciously (so he said) flogged
out of it by Boyer. And meantime he was reading
metaphysics, and writing verses, in the true spirit of the
future Coleridge. The lines he composed in his sixteenth
year, suggested by his habit of living in the future till
time present and future became in thought inextricably

intermingled, surely entitle him to the name of the
"marvellous boy," as truly as anything Chatterton had
written at the same age :—

> On the wide level of a mountain's head
> (I knew not where, but 'twas some fairy place)
> Their pinions, ostrich-like, for sails outspread,
> Two lovely children run an endless race,
>   A sister and a brother!
>   That far outstripp'd the other;
> Yet ever runs she with reverted face,
> And looks and listens for the boy behind;
>   For he, alas! is blind!
> O'er rough and smooth with even step he pass'd,
> And knows not whether he be first or last.

A striking feature of these lines is not so much that they
are not the echo of any one school of poetry, but that in
the special *metaphysic* of the thought, and the peculiar
witchery of the verse, Coleridge here anticipated his
maturest powers. It is on first thoughts strange that the
boy who had read through whole libraries, "folios and
all," and who could write verses such as these, should have
been so deeply stirred as we know him to have been at
the age of seventeen, when the small volume of fourteen
sonnets of William Lisle Bowles fell into his hands.
What was there, it might well be asked, in the poetry of
Bowles, pathetic and graceful as it was, so to quicken the
poetic impulse of Coleridge, that years afterwards he wrote
of it to a friend as having "done his heart more good
than all the other books he ever read, excepting his Bible."
It is the fashion in the present day to speak slightingly
of Bowles, but his sonnets have unquestionable merit.
Their language is melodious to a degree which perhaps
only Collins in that century had surpassed, and it expressed a tender melancholy, which may have been

inspired also by the study of the same poet. But Coleridge,
the omnivorous reader, can hardly have been unacquainted
with Gray and Collins, and the writer of such lines as—

> On the wide level of a mountain's head
> (I knew not where, but 'twas some fairy place),

could have had little to learn, as to the subtler music of
versification, even from the greatest models. But it is
significant that Coleridge couples these sonnets with the
Bible, and he could hardly have done so without meaning
it to be understood that Bowles' sonnets marked some
change not purely artistic in his mind's growth. For
the melancholy of Gray was constitutional, but the
sadness of Bowles had its root in a close habit of in-
trospection, and dwelling upon the moral side of things.
The pensive beauty of such a sonnet as the well-known
one on the *Influence of Time on Grief* wakes chords that
are not often reached by the sentiment of the elder poets.
There can be little doubt that at a critical point of
Coleridge's life his moral nature was touched in ways for
which he was profoundly grateful by these few poems of
Bowles. He admits the obligation, indeed, in the first
version of his sonnet to Bowles, when he confesses that
"those soft strains" waked in him "love and sympathy"
as well as fancy, and made him henceforth "not callous
to a brother's pains." And we are justified in believing
that his young companion, Charles Lamb, was passing
with him along the same path of deepening thoughtfulness.
He, too, had felt the charm of Bowles' tenderness. In
his earliest letters to Coleridge no other name is mentioned oftener and with more admiration ; and writing
to his friend a few years later, from the "drudgery of the
desk's dead wood " at the India House, Lamb complains

sorrowfully, "Not a soul loves Bowles here: scarce one
has heard of Burns: few but laugh at me for reading my
Testament."

It was in the year 1789, the year of the publication of
Bowles' earliest sonnets, that Charles Lamb was removed
from Christ's Hospital, and the companionship of the two
friends was for a while interrupted. Lamb had found
other congenial associates among the Blue Coats, and has
embalmed their names in various ways in his essays; the
two Le Grices from Cornwall, and James White, whose
passion was for Shakespeare, and who afterwards compiled
a collection of letters, as between Falstaff and his friends,
in which he displayed some fancy, but chiefly a certain
skill in taking to pieces the phraseology of the humorous
characters in the historical plays and re-setting it in
divers combinations. It was by these and other like
accidents that the tastes and powers of the young Charles
Lamb were being drawn forth in those seven years of
school-life. The Latin and Greek of the Rev. Matthew
Field, the under grammar-master, even the more advanced
instruction under James Boyer, had a less important
bearing on the future *Elia* than the picturesque surroundings of the Temple, alternating with those of the foundation of Edward VI., and above all, the daily companionship of Samuel Taylor Coleridge.

Leigh Hunt, in his autobiography, has described with
great humour and spirit the Christ's Hospital of his day,
only two or three years later. Hunt left school at the age
of fifteen, when he had attained the same rank as Lamb—
deputy Grecian—and, as he tells us, for the same reason.
He, too, had an impediment in his speech. "I did not
stammer half so badly as I used, but it was understood that
a Grecian was bound to deliver a public speech before he

left school, and to go into the Church afterwards; and as
I could do neither of these things, a Grecian I could not
be." During his seven years in the school, Hunt often
saw Charles Lamb, when he came to visit his old school-
fellows, and recalled in after-life the " pensive, brown,
handsome, and kindly face," and "the gait advancing with
a motion from side to side, between involuntary uncon-
sciousness and attempted ease." He dressed even then,
Leigh Hunt adds, with that " Quaker-like plainness " that
distinguished him all through life.

To leave school must have been to Charles Lamb a
bitter sorrow. His aptitude for the special studies
of the school was undeniable, and to part from Coleridge
must have been a still heavier blow. His biographers
have followed Leigh Hunt in pointing out that the school
exhibitions to the universities were given on the implied
condition of the winners of them proceeding to holy orders,
and that in Lamb's case his infirmity of speech made that
impossible. But there were probably other reasons, not
less cogent. It must have been of importance to his
family that Charles should, with as little delay as possible,
begin to earn his bread. There was poverty in his home,
and the prospect of means becoming yet more straitened.
There were deepening anxieties of still graver cast, as we
shall see hereafter. The youngest child of the family
returned to share this poverty and these anxieties, and to
learn thus early the meaning of that law of sacrifice to
which he so cheerfully submitted for the remainder of his
life.

CHAPTER II.

FAMILY STRUGGLES AND SORROWS.

(1789—1796.)

IN two of Lamb's Essays of Elia, *My Relations*, and *Mackery End in Hertfordshire*, he has described various members of his own family, and among them his brother John and his sister Mary. These should be carefully read, in conjunction with the less studied utterances on the same theme in his letters, by those who would understand the conditions of that home of which he now became an inmate. Of the family of seven children born in the Temple to John and Elizabeth Lamb, only three survived, the two just mentioned, and Charles. The elder brother, John, at the time of his brother's leaving school a young man of twenty-six, held an appointment in the South Sea House. There was a Plumer in the office, mentioned by Lamb in his essay on that institution, and it was with the Plumer family in Hertfordshire that Lamb's grandmother had been housekeeper. It was probably to such an introduction that John Lamb owed his original clerkship in the office, and it is evident that at the time he first comes under our notice, his position in the office was fairly lucrative, and that the young man, unmarried, and of pleasant artistic tastes, was living by himself, enjoying life, and not

C

troubling himself too much about his poor relations in the Temple. The genial selfishness of his character is described with curious frankness by Charles, who yet seemed to entertain a kind of admiration for the well-dressed dilettante who cast in this way a kind of reflected light of respectability upon his humble relatives. He even addresses a sonnet to his brother, and applauds him for keeping "the elder brother up in state." There is a touch of sarcasm here, perhaps; and there is a sadder vein of irony in the description in *My Relations :*—

It does me good as I walk towards the street of my daily avoca-tion on some fine May morning, to meet him marching in a quite opposite direction, with a jolly handsome presence, and shining sanguine face that indicates some purchase in his eye—a Claude or a Hobbima—for much of his enviable leisure is consumed at Christie's and Phillips', or where not, to pick up pictures and such gauds. On these occasions he mostly stoppeth me, to read a short lecture on the advantage a person like me possesses above himself, in having his time occupied with business which he *must do ;* assureth me that he often feels it hang heavy on his hands; wishes he had fewer holidays; and goes off West-ward Ho! chanting a tune to Pall Mall; perfectly convinced that he has convinced me, while I proceed in my opposite direction tuneless.

We feel that this picture needs no additional touches. "Marching in a quite opposite direction" was what John Lamb continued to do, in all respects, as concerned the dutiful and home-keeping members of his family. It was not to him that father and mother, sister or brother, were to look for help in their great need. Wholly different was the other elder child, next to him in age, Mary Lamb, the *Bridget Elia* of the Essays. Ten years older than Charles, she filled a position to him in these boyish days

rather of mother than of sister.   It is clear that these two
children from the earliest age depended much on one
another for sympathy and support.   The mother never
understood or appreciated the daughter's worth, and the
father, who seems to have married late in life, was
already failing in health and powers when Charles left
school.   The brother and sister were therefore thrown
upon one another for companionship and intellectual
sympathy, when school friendships were for a while sus-
pended.   Mary Lamb shared from childhood her brother's
taste for reading.   " She was tumbled early, by accident
or design, into a spacious closet of good old English
reading, without much selection or prohibition, and
browsed at will upon that fair and wholesome pasturage."
The spacious closet was, it would seem, the library of
Samuel Salt, to which both she and Charles early had
access.   It was a blessed resource for them in face of
the monotony and other discomforts of their home and
against more serious evils.   There was, as we have seen,
a taint of mania in the family, inherited from the father's
side.   It appeared in different shapes in all three children, if we are to trust a casual remark in one of Charles'
letters touching his brother John.   But in Mary Lamb
there is reason to suppose that it had been a cause of
anxiety to her parents from an early period of her life.   In
one of his earliest poems addressed to Charles Lamb,
Coleridge speaks of him creeping round a " dear-loved
sister's bed, with noiseless step," soothing each pang with
fond solicitude.   These claims upon his brotherly watch-
fulness fell to the lot of Charles while still a boy, and
they were never relaxed during life.   There was a
pathetic truth in the prediction of Coleridge which followed :—

Cheerily, dear Charles !
Thou thy best friend shalt cherish many a year.

He continued to devote himself to this, his best friend, for
more than forty years, and henceforth the lives of the
brother and sister are such that the story of the one can
hardly be told apart from the other.

It has been said that Lamb's first years were passed
between the Temple and Christ's Hospital — between
" cloister and cloister "—but there were happy holiday
seasons when he had glimpses of a very different life.
These were spent with his grandmother, Mary Field, at
the old mansion of the Plumer family, Blakesware, closely
adjoining the pleasant village of Widford, in Hertfordshire. The Plumers had two residences in the county,
one at Gilston, and the other just mentioned, a few miles
distant. The latter was the house where the dowager
Mrs. Plumer and younger children of the family resided. Sometimes there would be no members of the
family to inhabit it, and at such times old Mrs. Field, who
held the post of housekeeper for the last fifty or sixty
years of her life, reigned supreme over the old place. Her
three grandchildren were then often with her, and the
old-fashioned mansion, with its decaying tapestries and
carved chimneys, together with the tranquil, rural beauty
of the gardens and the surrounding country, made an
impression on the childish imagination of Lamb, which
is not to be overlooked in considering the influences which
moulded his thought and style. There were many ties of
family affection binding him to Hertfordshire. His
grandmother was a native of the county, and in the beautiful essay called *Mackery End* he has described a visit
paid in later life to other relations, in the neighbourhood
of Wheathampstead. It is noticeable how Lamb, the

"scorner of the fields," as Wordsworth termed him, yet
showed the true poet's appreciation of English rural
scenery, whenever at least his heart was touched by any
association of it with human joy or sorrow.

In 1792 Mrs. Field died at a good old age, and lies
buried in the quiet churchyard of Widford. Lamb has
preserved her memory in the tender tribute to her virtues,
The Grandame, which appeared among his earliest published
verses,—

> On the green hill top
> Hard by the house of prayer, a modest roof
> And not distinguished from its neighbour-barn
> Save by a slender tapering length of spire,
> The Grandame sleeps. A plain stone barely tells
> The name and date to the chance passenger.

Time and weather have effaced even name and date, but
the stone is still pointed out in Widford churchyard. The
old lady had suffered long from an incurable disease, and
the young Charles Lamb had clearly found some of his
earliest religious impressions deepened by watching her
courage and resignation :—

> For she had studied patience in the school
> Of Christ ; much comfort she had thence derived
> And was a *follower* of the Nazarene.

With her death the tie with Blakesware was not broken.
The family of the Lambs had pleasant relations with other
of the Widford people. Their constant friend, Mr. Randal Norris, the Sub-treasurer of the Inner Temple, had
connexions with the place, and long after the death of Mrs.
Field we find Lamb and his sister spending occasional
holidays in the neighbourhood.

At some date, unfixed, in the two years following his

removal from Christ's Hospital, Charles obtained a post of
some kind in the South Sea House, where his brother John
held an appointment. No account of this period of his life
remains to us, except such as can be drawn from the
essay on the *South Sea House*, written thirty years later in
the *London Magazine* as the first of the papers signed
Elia. The essay contains little or nothing about himself,
and we are ignorant as to the duties and emoluments of
his situation. It was not long, however, before he got
promotion, in the form of a clerkship in the accountant's
office of the East India Company, obtained for him through
the influence of Samuel Salt. His salary began at the
rate of 70*l.* a year, rising by gradual steps, and in the service
of the East India Company Charles Lamb continued for
the rest of his working life.

Of these first years of official life, from the date of his
entry into the office in April, 1792, till the spring of 1796,
there is little to be learned, save from a few scattered
allusions in the letters which from this later date have
been preserved. Up to the year 1795 the family of Lamb
continued to live in the Temple, when the increasing
infirmity of John Lamb the elder made him leave the
service of his old employer, and retire on a small pension
to lodgings in Little Queen Street, Holborn. No fragment
of writing of Charles Lamb of earlier date than 1795 has
been preserved. His work as a junior clerk absorbed the
greater part of his day and of his year. In his first
years of service his annual holiday was a single week, and
this scanty breathing-space he generally spent in his
favourite Hertfordshire. Then there were the occasional
visits to the theatre, and it was the theatre which all
through life shared with books the keenest love of Lamb
and his sister. He has left us an account, in the essay,

My First Play, of his earliest experiences of this kind, beginning with *Artaxerxes*, and proceeding to *The Lady of the Manor* and the *Way of the World*, all seen by him when he was between six and seven years old. Seven years elapsed before he saw another play (for play-going was not permitted to Christ's Hospital boys), and he admits that when after that interval he visited the theatre again, much of its former charm had vanished. The old classical tragedy and the old-world sentimental comedy alike failed to satisfy him, and it was not till he first saw Mrs. Siddons that the acted drama reasserted its power. "The theatre became to him, once more," he tells us, "the most delightful of recreations." One of the earliest of his sonnets records the impression made upon him by this great actress. And as soon as we are admitted through his correspondence with Coleridge and others to know his tastes and habits, we find how important a part the drama and all its associations were playing in the direction of his genius.

Nor was the gloom of his home life unrelieved by occasional renewals of the intellectual companionship he had enjoyed at school. Coleridge had gone up to Jesus College, Cambridge, early in 1791, and except during the six months of his soldier's life in the Light Dragoons, remained there for the next four years. During this time he made occasional visits to London, when it was the great pleasure of the two school-fellows to meet at a tavern near Smithfield, the "Salutation and Cat" (probably a well-known rallying-point in the old Christ's days), and there to spend long evenings in discussion on literature and the other topics dear to both. Coleridge was now writing poems, and finding a temporary home for them in the columns of the *Morning Chronicle*. Among them

appeared the sonnet on Mrs. Siddons, which was thus
probably Lamb's first appearance in print. Both the
young men were clearly dreaming of authorship, and
Lamb's first avowed appearance as author was in the first
volume of poems by Coleridge, published by Cottle, of
Bristol, in the spring of the year 1796. "The effusions
signed C. L.," says Coleridge in the preface to this volume,
"were written by Mr. Charles Lamb of the India House.
Independently of the signature, their superior merit would
have sufficiently distinguished them." The effusions
consisted of four sonnets, the one already noticed on Mrs.
Siddons, one "written at midnight by the sea-side after a
voyage," and two, in every way the most noteworthy,
dealing with the one love-romance of Charles Lamb's life.
The sonnets have no special literary value, but the first of
these has importance enough in its bearing on Lamb's
character to justify quotation :—

> Was it some sweet device of Faëry
> That mocked my steps with many a lonely glade,
> And fancied wanderings with a fair-haired maid ?
> Have these things been ?   Or what rare witchery,
> Impregning with delights the charmed air,
> Enlightened up the semblance of a smile
> In those fine eyes ? methought they spake the while
> Soft soothing things, which might enforce despair
> To drop the murdering knife, and let go by
> His foul resolve.   And does the lonely glade
> Still court the footsteps of the fair-haired maid ?
> Still in her locks the gales of summer sigh ?
> While I forlorn do wander, reckless where,
> And 'mid my wanderings meet no Anna there.

If the allusions in this and the following sonnet stood
alone, we might well be asking, as in the case of Shakespeare's sonnets, whether the situation was not dramatic

rather than autobiographical; but we have good reasons
for inferring that the Anna, "the fair-haired maid" of
these poems, had a real existence. His first love is referred
to constantly in later letters and essays as Alice W——n,
and it is easy to perceive that the Anna of the sonnets
and this Alice W——n were the same person. In both
cases the fair hair and the mild, pale blue eyes are the
salient features. But the sonnets that tell of these, tell
also of the "winding wood-walks green," and

> the little cottage which she loved,
> The cottage which did once my all contain.

From these alone we might infer that Lamb had
first met the subject of them, not in London, but
during his frequent visits to Blakesware. Lamb himself, often so curiously out-spoken on the subject
of his personal history, has nowhere directly told us
where he met his Alice, but he cannot seriously have
meant to keep the secret. In the essay, *Blakesmoor in
H——shire*, he recalls the picture-gallery with the old
family portraits, and among them "that beauty with the
cool, blue, pastoral drapery, and a lamb, that hung next
the great bay window, with the bright yellow Hertfordshire hair, *so like my Alice!*" His "fair-haired maid"
was clearly from Hertfordshire. It will be seen hereafter
what light is further thrown on the matter by Lamb himself. All that we know as certain, is that Lamb, while
yet a boy, lost his heart, and that whether the course of
true love ran smooth or not, he willingly submitted to
forego the hoped-for tie, when a claim upon his devotion
appeared in the closer circle of his home.

Unless, indeed, a more personal and even more terrible
occasion of this sacrifice had arisen at an earlier date. We

know, on his own admission, that in the winter of 1795-96,
Charles Lamb himself succumbed to the family malady,
and passed some weeks in confinement.   In the earliest
of his letters that has been preserved, belonging to the
early part of 1796, he tells his friend Coleridge the sad
truth :—

My life has been somewhat diversified of late. The six weeks
that finished last year and began this, your very humble servant
spent very agreeably in a madhouse at Hoxton. I am got somewhat rational now, and don't bite any one. But mad I was ! . . . .
Coleridge, it may convince you of my regard for you when I tell
you my head ran on you in my madness, as much almost as on
another person, who I am inclined to think was the more
immediate cause of my temporary frenzy.

The " other person " can have been no other than the
fair-haired Alice, and if disappointed love was the immediate cause of his derangement, the discovery in him of
this tendency may have served to break off all relations
between the lovers still more effectually.   Wonderfully
touching are the lines which, as he tells Coleridge in the
same letter, were written by him in his prison-house in
one of his lucid intervals :—

TO MY SISTER.

If from my lips some angry accents fell,
Peevish complaint, or harsh reproof unkind,
'Twas but the error of a sickly mind
And troubled thoughts, clouding the purer well,
And waters clear, of Reason : and for me
Let this my verse the poor atonement be—
My verse, which thou to praise wert e'er inclined
Too highly, and with a partial eye to see
No blemish.   Thou to me didst ever show
Kindest affection ; and would'st oft-times lend

An ear to the despairing, love sick lay,
Weeping my sorrows with me, who repay
But ill the mighty debt of love I owe,
Mary, to thee, my sister and my friend.

The history of many past weeks or months seems
written in these lines; the history of a hopeless attachment, a reason yielding to long distress of mind, and a
sister's love already repaying by anticipation the " mighty
debt " which in after days it was itself to owe.

This year 1795-96, was indeed a memorable one in the
annals of the brother and sister. The fortunes of the
Lamb family were at low ebb. They had removed to
lodgings in Little Queen Street, the mother a confirmed
invalid, and the father sinking gradually into second childhood. Charles had been temporarily under restraint, and
Mary Lamb, in addition to the increasing labour of minis-
tering to her parents, was working for their common
maintenance by taking in needlework. It is not strange
that under this pressure her own reason, so often
threatened, at last gave way. It was in September
of 1796 that the awful calamity of her life befell. A
young apprentice girl, who was at work in the common sitting-room while dinner was preparing, appears to
have excited the latent mania. Mary Lamb seized a
knife from the table, pursued the girl round the room,
and finally stabbed to the heart her mother who had interfered in the girl's behalf. It was Charles Lamb himself who seized the unhappy sister, and wrested the knife
from her hand, but not before she had hurled in her
rage other knives about the room, and wounded, though
not fatally, the now almost imbecile father. *The Times* of
a few days later relates that an inquest was held on
the following day, and a verdict of insanity returned in

the case of the unhappy daughter. Lamb's account of the event is given in a letter to Coleridge, of Sept. 27th.

MY DEAREST FRIEND,—White, or some of my friends, or the public papers by this time may have informed you of the terrible calamities that have fallen on our family. I will only give you the outlines :—My poor dear, dearest sister, in a fit of insanity, has been the death of her own mother. I was at hand only time enough to snatch the knife out of her grasp. She is at present in a madhouse, from whence I fear she must be moved to an hospital. God has preserved to me my senses—I eat, and drink, and sleep, and have my judgment, I believe, very sound. My poor father was slightly wounded, and I am left to take care of him and my aunt. Mr. Norris, of the Bluecoat School, has been very kind to us, and we have no other friend ; but, thank God, I am very calm and composed, and able to do the best that remains to do. Write as religious a letter as possible, but no mention of what is gone and done with. With me the "former things are passed away," and I have something more to do than to feel.

God Almighty have us well in His keeping.

C. LAMB.

Mention nothing of poetry. I have destroyed every vestige of past vanities of that kind. Do as you please ; but if you publish, publish mine (I give free leave) without name or initial, and never send me a book, I charge you.

A second letter followed in less than a week, in a tone somewhat less forlorn.

Your letter was an inestimable treasure to me. It will be a comfort to you, I know, to know that our prospects are somewhat brighter. My poor dear, dearest sister, the unhappy and unconscious instrument of the Almighty's judgments on our house, is restored to her senses ; to a dreadful sense and recollection of what has past, awful to her mind and impressive (as it must be to the end of life), but tempered with religious resignation and

the reasonings of a sound judgment, which, in this early stage,
knows how to distinguish between a deed committed in a tran-
sient fit of frenzy, and the terrible guilt of a mother's murder. I
have seen her. I found her, this morning calm and serene;
far, very far, from an indecent, forgetful serenity; she has a
most affectionate and tender concern for what has happened.
Indeed, from the beginning, frightful and hopeless as her disorder seemed, I had confidence enough in her strength of mind
and religious principle, to look forward to a time when *even she*
might recover tranquillity. God be praised, Coleridge, wonderful as it is to tell, I have never once been otherwise than collected and calm; even on the dreadful day, and in the midst of
the terrible scene, I preserved a tranquillity which bystanders
may have construed into indifference—a tranquillity not of
despair. Is it folly or sin in me to say that it was a religious
principle that *most* supported me? I allow much to other
favourable circumstances. I felt that I had something else to
do than to regret. On that first evening, my aunt was lying in-
sensible, to all appearance like one dying,—my father, with his
poor forehead plastered over, from a wound he had received from
a daughter dearly loved by him, who loved him no less dearly,—
my mother a dead and murdered corpse in the next room,—yet
was I wonderfully supported. I closed not my eyes in sleep that
night, but lay without terrors and without despair. I have lost
no sleep since. I had been long used not to rest in things of
sense; had endeavoured after a comprehension of mind, unsatisfied with the "ignorant present time," and this kept me up. I
had the whole weight of the family thrown on me; for my
brother, little disposed (I speak not without tenderness for him)
at any time to take care of old age and infirmities, had now, with
his bad leg, an exemption from such duties, and I was now
left alone. . . . .
    Our friends here have been very good. Sam Le Grice, who
was then in town, was with me the three or four first days, and
was as a brother to me; gave up every hour of his time, to the
very hurting of his health and spirits, in constant attendance
and humouring my poor father; talked with him, read to him,

played at cribbage with him (for so short is the old man's recollection that he was playing at cards, as though nothing had
happened, while the coroner's inquest was sitting over the way).
Samuel wept tenderly when he went away, for his mother wrote
him a very severe letter on his loitering so long in town, and he
was forced to go. Mr. Norris, of Christ's Hospital, has been as
a father to me; Mrs. Norris as a mother, though we had few
claims on them. A gentleman, brother to my godmother, from
whom we never had right or reason to expect any such assistance, sent my father 20l.; and to crown all these God's
blessings to our family at such a time, an old lady, a cousin
of my father's and aunt's, a gentlewoman of fortune, is to
take my aunt and make her comfortable for the short remainder of her days. My aunt is recovered, and as well as ever, and
highly pleased at thoughts of going; and has generously given
up the interest of her little money (which was formerly paid my
father for her board) wholly and solely to my sister's use.
Reckoning this, we have, Daddy and I, for our two selves and
an old maid-servant to look after him when I am out, which will
be necessary, 170l., or 180l. rather, a year, out of which we can
spare 50l. or 60l. at least for Mary while she stays at Islington,
where she must and shall stay during her father's life, for his
and her comfort. I know John will make speeches about it,
but she shall not go into an hospital. The good lady of the
madhouse, and her daughter—an elegant, sweet-behaved young
lady—love her and are taken with her amazingly; and I know
from her own mouth she loves them, and longs to be with them
as much. Poor thing! they say she was but the other morning
saying she knew she must go to Bethlehem for life; that one of
her brothers would have it so, but the other would wish it not,
but be obliged to go with the stream; that she had often as she
passed Bethlehem thought it likely, " here it may be my fate to
end my days," conscious of a certain flightiness in her poor
head oftentimes, and mindful of more than one severe illness of
that nature before. A legacy of 100l., which my father will
have at Christmas, and this 20l. I mentioned before, with what

is in the house, will much more than set us clear. If my father, an old servant-maid, and I, can't live, and live comfortably, on 130*l.* or 120*l.* a year, we ought to burn by slow fires; and I almost would, that Mary might not go into an hospital. Let me not leave one unfavourable impression on your mind respecting my brother. Since this has happened he has been very kind and brotherly, but I fear for his mind. He has taken his ease in the world, and is not fit himself to struggle with difficulties, nor has much accustomed himself to throw himself into their way; and I know his language is already, "Charles, you must take care of yourself, you must not abridge yourself of a single pleasure you have been used to," &c., &c., and in that style of talking. But you, a necessarian, can respect a difference of mind, and love what is amiable in a character not perfect. He has been very good, but I fear for his mind. Thank God, I can unconnect myself with him, and shall manage all my father's monies in future myself if I take charge of Daddy, which poor John has not even hinted a wish, at any future time even, to share with me. The lady at this madhouse assures me that I may dismiss immediately both doctor and apothecary, retaining occasionally a composing draught or so for a while; and there is a less expensive establishment in her house, where she will not only have a room and nurse to herself for 50*l.* or guineas a year— the outside would be 60*l.*—you know by economy how much more even I shall be able to spare for her comforts. She will, I fancy, if she stays make one of the family, rather than of the patients; the old and young ladies I like exceedingly, and she loves dearly; and they, as the saying is, take to her extraordinarily, if it is extraordinary that people who see my sister should love her. Of all the people I ever saw in the world, my poor sister was most and thoroughly devoid of the quality of selfishness. I will enlarge upon her qualities, dearest soul, in a future letter for my own comfort, for I understand her thoroughly; and if I mistake not, in the most trying situation that a human being can be found in, she will be found (I speak not with sufficient humility, I fear, but humanly and foolishly speaking) she will be found, I trust, uniformly great and amiable. God keep her in her present mind, to whom be thanks and praise for all His dispensations to mankind.

It is necessary for the full understanding of what Charles Lamb was, and of the life that lay before him, that this deeply interesting account should be given in his own words. Anything that a biographer might add would only weaken the picture of courage, dutifulness and affection here presented. The only fitting sequel to it is the history of the remaining five-and-thirty years in which he fulfilled so nobly and consistently his self-imposed task.

That task was made lighter to him than in the natural dejection of the first sad moments he could have dared to hope. The poor old father survived the mother but a few months, and passed quietly out of life early in the following year. The old aunt, who did not long find a home with the capricious relative who had undertaken the charge of her, returned to Charles and his father, only, however, to survive her brother a few weeks. Charles was now free to consult his own wishes as to the future care of his sister. She was still in the asylum at Hoxton, and it was his earnest desire that she might return to live with him. By certain conditions and arrangements between him and the proper authorities, her release from confinement was ultimately brought about, and the brother's guardianship was accepted as sufficient for the future. She returned to share his solitude for the remainder of his life. The mania which had once attacked Charles, never in his case returned. Either the shock of calamity, or the controlling power of the vow he had laid on himself, overmastered the inherited tendency. But in the case of Mary Lamb it returned at frequent intervals through life, never again happily with any disastrous result. The attacks seem to have been generally attended with forewarnings, which enabled the brother and sister to take the necessary measures, and a friend of the Lambs has related how on one occasion he met the brother and sister, at such a season, walking hand in hand across the fields to the old asylum, both bathed in tears.

CHAPTER III.

(1796—1800.)

EARLY in 1797 Charles Lamb and his sister began their life of "dual loneliness." But during these first years the brother's loneliness was often unshared. Much of Mary Lamb's life was passed in visits to the asylum, and the mention of her successive attacks is of melancholy recurrence in Charles' letters. Happily for the brother's sanity of mind, he was beginning to find friends and sympathies in new directions. What books had been to him all his life, and what education he had been finding in them, is evident from his earliest extant letters. His published correspondence begins in 1796, with a letter to Coleridge, then at Bristol, and from this and other letters of the sameyear we see the first signs of that variety of literary taste so noteworthy in a young man of twenty-one. The letters of this year are mainly on critical subjects. He encloses his own sonnets, and points out the passages in elder writers, Parnell or Cowley, to which he has been indebted. Or he acknowledges poems of Coleridge, sent for his criticism, and proceeds to express his opinion on them with frankness. He had been introduced to Southey, by Coleridge, some time in 1795, and he writes to the latter, "With *Joan of Arc* I have been delighted, amazed ;

I had not presumed to expect anything of such excellence from Southey. Why, the poem is alone sufficient to redeem the character of the age we live in from the imputation of degenerating in poetry, were there no such beings extant as Burns, Bowles, and Cowper, and — ; fill up the blank how you please." It is noticeable also how prompt the young man was to discover the real significance of the poetic revival of the latter years of the eighteenth century. Burns he elsewhere mentions at this time to Coleridge in stronger terms of enthusiam as having been the "God of my idolatry, as Bowles was of yours," nor was he less capable of appreciating the "divine chitchat" of Cowper. The real greatness of Wordsworth he was one of the earliest to discover and to proclaim. And at the same time his imagination was being stirred by the romantic impulse that was coming from Germany. "Have you read," he asks Coleridge, "the ballad called 'Leonora' in the second number of the *Monthly Magazine?* If you have !!! There is another fine song, from the same author (Bürger) in the third number, of scarce inferior merit." But still more remarkable in the intellectual history of so young a man is the acquaintance he shows with the earlier English authors, at a time when the revival of Shakespearian study was comparatively recent, and when the other Elizabethan dramatists were all but unknown save to the archæologist. We must suppose that the library of Samuel Salt was more than usually rich in old folios, for certainly Lamb had not only 'browsed' (to use his own expression), but had read and criticized deeply, as well as discursively. In a letter to Coleridge of this same year, 1796, he quotes with enthusiasm the rather artificial lines of Massinger in *A very Woman*, pointing out the "fine effect of the double endings."

Not far from where my father lives, a lady,
A neighbour by, blest with as great a beauty
As nature durst bestow without undoing,
Dwelt, and most happily, as I thought then,
And blest the house a thousand times she dwelt in.
This beauty, in the blossom of my youth,
When my first fire knew no adulterate incense,
Nor I no way to flatter but my fondness,
In all the bravery my friends could show me,
In all the faith my innocence could give me,
In the best language my true tongue could tell me,
And all the broken sighs my sick heart lend me,
I sued and served ; long did I serve this lady,
Long was my travail, long my trade to win her ;
With all the duty of my soul I served her.[1]

Beaumont and Fletcher he quotes with no less delight,
"in which authors I can't help thinking there is a
greater richness of poetical fancy than in any one, Shakespeare excepted." Again, he asks the same inseparable
friend, "Among all your quaint readings did you ever
light upon *Walton's Complete Angler?* I asked you
the question once before ; it breathes the very spirit of
innocence, purity, and simplicity of heart ; there are many
choice old verses interspersed in it : it would sweeten a
man's temper at any time to read it : it would Christianize
every discordant angry passion." And while thus discursive in his older reading, he was hardly less so in the
literature of his own century. He had been fascinated by
the *Confessions* of Rousseau, and was for a time at least
under the influence of the sentimental school of novelists,
the followers of Richardson and Sterne in England. So
varied was the field of authors and subjects on which his
style was being formed and his fancy nourished.

1 These lines are interesting as having been chosen by Lamb
for a "motto" to his first published poems. As so used, they
clearly bore a reference to his own patient wooing at that time.

Long afterwards, in his essay on *Books and Reading*, he boasted that he could read anything which he called *a book.* " I have no repugnances. Shaftesbury is not too genteel for me, nor Jonathan Wild too low." But this versatility of sympathy, which was at the root of so large a part of both matter and manner when he at length discovered where his real strength lay, had the effect of delaying that discovery for some time. His first essays in literature were mainly imitative, and though there is not one of them that is without his peculiar charm, or that a lover of Charles Lamb would willingly let die, they are more interesting from the fact of their author-ship, and from the light they throw on the growth of Lamb's mind, than for their intrinsic value.

Meantime, his life in the lonely Queen Street lodging was cheered by the acquisition of some new friends, chiefly introduced by Coleridge. He had known Southey since 1795, and some time in the following year, or early in 1797, he had formed a closer bond of sympathy with Charles Lloyd, son of a banker of Birmingham, a young man of poetic taste and melancholy temperament, who had taken up his abode, for the sake of intellectual compa-nionship, with Coleridge at Bristol. One of the first results of this companionship was a second literary venture in which the new friend took a share. A second edition of *Poems by S. T. Coleridge, to which are now added Poems by Charles Lamb and Charles Lloyd,* appeared at Bristol, in the summer of 1797, published by Coleridge's devoted admirer, Joseph Cottle.

" There were inserted in my former edition," writes Coleridge in the preface, " a few sonnets of my friend and old school-fellow, Charles Lamb. He has now communi-cated to me a complete collection of all his poems ; quæ

qui non prorsus amet, illum omnes et virtutes et veneres
odere." The phrase is a trifle grandiloquent to describe
the short list—some fifteen in all—of sonnets and occasional verses here printed. Nor is there anything in
their style to indicate the influence of new models. A
tender grace of the type of his old favourite, Bowles,
is still their chief merit, and they are interesting as
showing how deeply the events of the past few years had
stirred the religious side of Charles Lamb's nature. A
review of the day characterized the manner of Lamb and
Lloyd as "plaintive," and the epithet is not ill-chosen.
Lamb was still living chiefly in the past, and the thought
of his sister, and recollection of the pious "Grandame"
in Hertfordshire, with kindred memories of his own
childhood and disappointed affections, make the subject-
matter of almost all the verse. A little allegorical poem,
with the title of "A Vision of Repentance," relegated
to an appendix in this same volume, marks the most
sacred confidence that Lamb ever gave to the world as to
his meditations on the mystery of evil.

It is unlikely that this little venture brought any
profit to its authors, or that a subsequent volume of blank
verse by Lamb and Lloyd in the following year was more
remunerative. To Lloyd the question was doubtless of
less importance ; but Lamb was anxious for his sister's
sake to add to his scanty income, and with this view he
resolved to make an experiment in prose fiction. In the
year 1798 he composed his little story, bearing the title,
as originally issued, of *A Tale of Rosamund Gray and Old
Blind Margaret*.

This "miniature romance," as Talfourd calls it, is perhaps better known after the essays of Elia, than any of
Lamb's writings, and the secret of its charm, in the face

of improbabilities and unrealities of many kinds, is one of
the curiosities of literature. The story itself is built up
of the most heterogeneous materials. The idea of the
story, the ruin of a village maiden, Rosamund Gray, by a
melodramatic villain with the "uncommon" name of
Matravis, was suggested to Lamb, as he admits in a letter
to Southey, by a "foolish" (and it must be added, a very
scurrilous) old ballad about "an old woman clothed in
grey." The name of his heroine he borrowed from some
verses of his friend Lloyd's (not included in their joint
volume), and that of the villain from one of the ruffians
employed to murder the king in Marlowe's *Edward the
Second*,—that death-scene which he afterwards told the
world "moved pity and terror beyond any scene ancient
or modern" with which he was acquainted. The conduct
of the little story bears strong traces of the influence of
Richardson and Mackenzie, and a rather forced reference
to the latter's *Julia de Roubigné* seems to show where he
had lately been reading. A portion of the narrative is
conducted by correspondence between the two well-bred
young ladies of the story, and when one of them begins a
letter to her cousin, "Health, innocence, and beauty shall
be thy bridesmaids, my sweet cousin," we are at once
aware in what school of polite letter-writing the author
had studied. After the heroine, the two principal characters are a brother and sister, Allan and Elinor Clare,
the relation between whom (the sister is represented as
just ten years older than her brother) is borrowed almost
without disguise from that of Lamb and his sister Mary.
"Elinor Clare was the best good creature, the least selfish
human being I ever knew, always at work for other
people's good, planning other people's happiness, continually forgetful to consult for her own personal gratifica-

tions, except indirectly in the welfare of another; while
her parents lived, the most attentive of daughters; since
they died, the kindest of sisters. I never knew but *one*
like her." There is besides a schoolfellow of Allan's, who
precedes him to college, evidently a recollection of the
school-friendship with Coleridge. But still more significant as showing the personal element in the little
romance, is the circumstance that Lamb lays the scene of
it in that Hertfordshire village of Widford where so many
of his own happiest hours had been spent, and that the
heroine, Rosamund Gray, is drawn with those features on
which he was never weary of dwelling in the object of his
own boyish passion. Rosamund, with the pale blue eyes
and the "yellow Hertfordshire hair" is but a fresh copy
of his Anna and his Alice. That Rosamund Gray had
an actual counterpart in real life seems certain, and the
little group of cottages, in one of which she dwelt with
her old grandmother, is still shown in the village of Widford, about half a mile from the site of the old mansion of
Blakesware. And it is the tradition of the village, and
believed by those who have the best means of judging,
that "Rosamund Gray" (her real name was equally
remote from this, and from Alice W——n) was Charles
Lamb's first and only love. Her fair hair and eyes, her
goodness, and (we may assume) her poverty, were drawn
from life. The rest of the story in which she bears a part
is of course pure fiction. The real Anna of the sonnets
made a prosperous marriage, and lived to a good old
age.

As if Lamb were resolved to give his little tale the
character of personal "confessions," he has contrived to
introduce into it, by quotation or allusion, all his favourite
writers, from Walton and Wither to Mackenzie and Burns.

But of more interest from this point of view than any resemblances of detail, is the shadow, as of recent calamity, that rests upon the story, and the strain of religious emotion that pervades it. It is this that gives the romance, conventional as it is for the most part in its treatment of life and manners, its real attractiveness. It is redolent of Lamb's native sweetness of heart, delicacy of feeling, and undefinable charm of style. And these qualities did not altogether fail to attract attention. The little venture was a moderate success, and brought its author some " few guineas." One tribute to its merits was paid many years later, which, we may hope, did not fail to reach the author. Shelley, writing to Leigh Hunt from Leghorn, in 1819, and acknowledging the receipt of a parcel of books, adds, " With it came, too, Lamb's works. What a lovely thing is his *Rosamund Gray* ! How much knowledge of the sweetest and deepest part of our nature in it ! When I think of such a mind as Lamb's, when I see how unnoticed remain things of such exquisite and complete perfection, what should I hope for myself, if I had not higher objects in view than fame ? "

There is scanty material for the biographer of Lamb and his sister during these first four years of struggling poverty. The few events that varied their monotonous life are to be gathered from the letters to Coleridge and Southey, written during this period. The former was married, and living at Nether Stowey, near Bristol, where Charles and Mary Lamb paid him apparently their first visit, during one of Charles' short holidays in the summer of 1797. This visit was made memorable by a slight accident that befell Coleridge on the day of their arrival, and forced him to remain at home while his visitors explored the surrounding country. Left alone in his garden, he composed the

curiously Wordsworthian lines, bearing for title (he was
perhaps reminded of Ferdinand in the *Tempest*), "This
lime-tree bower my prison," in which he apostrophizes
Lamb as the "gentle-hearted Charles," and addresses him
as one who had—

> Hungered after nature, many a year
> In the great city pent, winning thy way
> With sad and patient zeal, through evil and pain
> And strange calamity.

Charles did not quite relish the epithet "gentle-hearted,"
and showed that he winced under a title that savoured a
little of pity or condescension. Indeed, it is evident, in
spite of the real affection that Lamb never ceased to feel
for Coleridge, that the relations between the friends were
often strained during these earlier days. This year, 1797,
was that of the joint volume, and the mutual criticism
indulged so freely by both was leaving a little soreness
behind. Then there was the question of precedence
between Lamb and Lloyd in this same volume, which was
settled in Lloyd's favour, not without a few pangs, confessed by Lamb himself. And when, in the following
year, Coleridge was on the eve of his visit to Germany
with the Wordsworths, a foolish message of his, "If Lamb
requires any knowledge, let him apply to me," had been
repeated to Lamb by some injudicious friend, and did not
tend to improve matters. Lamb retaliated by sending
Coleridge a grimly humorous list of "Theses quædam
Theologicæ," to be by him "defended or oppugned (or both)
at Leipsic or Göttingen." Numbers five and six in this
list may be given as a sample. "Whether the higher
order of Seraphim illuminati ever sneer?" "Whether
pure intelligences can love, or whether they can love anything besides pure intellect?" The rest are in the same

vein, and if they have any point at all, it must lie in an allusion to certain airs of lofty superiority in which Coleridge had indulged to the annoyance of his friend. There was a temporary soreness in the heart of Charles on parting with his old companion. There had been a grievance of the same kind before. It had been bitterly repented of, even in a flood of tears. To the beginning of this year, 1798, belong the touching verses composed in the same spirit of self-confession that has marked so much of his writing up to this period, about the "old familiar faces." In their earliest shape they are more directly auto-biographical. Lamb afterwards omitted the first stanza, and gave the lines a less personal character. The precise occasion of their being written seems uncertain, but the reference to the friend whom he had so nearly thrown away, in a moment of pique, is unmistakable.

Where are they gone, the old familiar faces?
I had a mother, but she died, and left me—
Died prematurely in a day of horrors—
All, all are gone, the old familiar faces.

I have had playmates, I have had companions
In my days of childhood, in my joyful school-days,
All, all are gone, the old familiar faces.

I have been laughing, I have been carousing,
Drinking late, sitting late, with my bosom cronies—
All, all are gone, the old familiar faces.

I loved a love once, fairest among women.
Closed are her doors on me, I must not see her—
All, all are gone, the old familiar faces.

I had a friend, a kinder friend has no man.
Like an ingrate, I left my friend abruptly!
Left him to muse on the old familiar faces.

Ghost-like I paced round the haunts of my childhood.
Earth seemed a desert I was bound to traverse,
Seeking to find the old familiar faces.

Friend of my bosom, thou more than a brother ;
Why wert not thou born in my father's dwelling,
So might we talk of the old familiar faces.

For some they have died, and some they have left me,
And some are taken from me, all are departed ;
All, all are gone, the old familiar faces.

The "friend of my bosom" was the new associate,
Lloyd, who seems for a time at least to have taken Coleridge's place as Lamb's special confidant. He, too, had
had his grievances against the " greater Ajax," and the two
humbler combatants, who had " come into battle under his
shield," found consolation at this time in one another.
Lloyd was moody and sensitive—even then a prey to the
melancholy which clung to him through life, and it was
well for Lamb that on Coleridge leaving England he had
some more genial companionship to take refuge in.
It was three years since he had made the acquaintance of
Southey.   In the summer of 1797 he and Lloyd had
passed a fortnight under his roof in Hampshire.   And
now that Coleridge was far away, it was Southey who
naturally took his place as literary adviser and confidant.

We gather from Lamb's letters to Southey, in 1798-99,
that this change of association for the time was good for
him.   Coleridge and Lloyd were of temperaments too
nearly akin to Lamb's to be wholly serviceable in these
days, when the calamities in his family still overshadowed
him.   The friendship of Southey, the healthy-natured,
the industrious, and the methodical, was a wholesome
change of atmosphere.   Southey was now living at West-

bury, near Bristol. Though only a few months Lamb's senior, he had been three years a married man, and was valiantly working to support his young wife by that craft of literature which he followed so patiently to his life's end. In this year, 1798, he was in his sweetest and most humorous ballad vein. It was the year of the *Well of St. Keyne* and the *Battle of Blenheim*, and other of those shorter pieces by which Southey will always be most widely known. He had not failed to discover Lamb's value as a critic, and each eclogue or ballad, as it is written, is submitted to his judgment. The result of this change of interest is shown in a marked difference of tone and style in Lamb's letters. He is less sad and meditative, and begins to exhibit that peculiar playfulness which we associate with the future Elia. One day he writes,— "My tailor has brought me home a new coat, lapelled, with a velvet collar. He assures me everybody wears velvet collars now. Some are born fashionable, some achieve fashion, and others, like your humble servant, have fashion thrust upon them." And his remarks on Southey's ode *To a Spider* (in which he justly notes the metre as its chief merit, and wonders that "Burns had not hit upon it" are followed by a discursive pleasantry having the true Elia ring, " I love this sort of poems that open a new intercourse with the most despised of the animal and insect race. I think this vein may be further opened. Peter Pindar hath very prettily apostrophized a fly; Burns hath his mouse and his louse; Coleridge, less successfully, hath made overtures of intimacy to a jackass, therein only following, at unresembling distance, Sterne and greater Cervantes. Besides these, I know of no other examples of breaking down the partition between us and our 'poor earth-born companions.'" And the suggestion that follows, that Southey should undertake a series of poems, with the object of awakening sympathy for animals too generally ill-treated or held in disgust, is most characteristic, both in matter and manner. Indeed it is in these earlier letters to Southey, rather than in his poetry or in *Rosamund Gray*, that Charles Lamb was feeling the way to his true place in literature. Already we observe a vein of reflectiveness and a curious felicity of style which owe nothing to any predecessor. And if his humour, even in his lightest moods, has a tinge of sadness, it is not to be accounted for only by the suffering he had passed through. It belonged in fact to the profound humanity of its author, to the circumstance that with him, as with all true humorists, humour was but one side of an acute and almost painful sympathy.

At the close of the year 1799 Coleridge returned from Germany, and the intercourse between the two friends was at once resumed, never again to be interrupted. Early in the year following Charles and his sister removed from the Queen Street lodging, where they had continued to reside since his mother's death, to Chapel Street, Pentonville. It appears from a letter of Charles to Coleridge, in the spring of 1800, that there was no alleviation of his burden of constant anxiety. The faithful old servant of many years had died, after a few days' illness, and Lamb writes, " Mary, in consequence of fatigue and anxiety, is fallen ill again, and I was obliged to remove her yesterday. I am left alone in a house with nothing but Hetty's dead body to keep me company. To-morrow I bury her, and then I shall be quite alone with nothing but a cat to remind me that the house has been full of living beings like myself. My heart is quite sunk, and I don't know where to look for relief. Mary will get better again, but

her constantly being liable to these attacks is dreadful;
nor is it the least of our evils that her case and all our
story is so well known around us. We are in a manner
marked. Excuse my troubling you, but I have nobody by
me to speak to me. I slept out last night, not being able
to endure the change and the stillness; but I did not
sleep well, and I must come back to my own bed. I am
going to try and get a friend to come and be with me to-
morrow. I am completely shipwrecked. My head is quite
bad. I almost wish that Mary were dead. God bless
you. Love to Sarah and little Hartley."

It is the solitary instance in which he allows us to see
his patience and hopefulness for a moment failing him.
That terrible sentence "we are in a manner *marked*" has
not perhaps received its due weight, in the estimate of
what the brother and sister were called upon to bear. It
seems certain that if they were not actually driven from
lodging to lodging, because the dreadful rumour of madness could not be shaken off, they were at least
shunned and kept at a distance wherever they went.
The rooms in Pentonville they soon received notice to
quit, and it was then that Charles turned, perhaps because
they were more quiet and secure from vulgar overlooking,
to the old familiar and dearly-loved surroundings of his
childhood. "I am going to change my lodgings," he
writes later in this same year to his Cambridge friend,
Manning, in a tone of cheerful looking-forward simply
marvellous, considering the immediate cause of the
removal. "I am going to change my lodgings, having
received a hint that it would be agreeable, at our Lady's
next feast. I have partly fixed upon most delectable
rooms, which look out (when you stand a tip-toe) over the
Thames and Surrey Hills, at the upper end of King's

Bench Walks in the Temple. There I shall have all the
privacy of a house without the encumbrance, and shall be
able to lock my friends out as often as I desire to hold free
converse with my immortal mind—for my present lodgings
resemble a minister's levée, I have so increased my acquaintance (as they call 'em) since I have resided in town.
Like the country mouse that had tasted a little of urbane
manners, I long to be nibbling my own cheese by my dear
self, without mouse-traps and time-traps. By my new
plan I shall be as airy, up four pair of stairs, as in the
country, and in a garden in the midst of enchanting (more
than Mahomedan paradise) London, whose dirtiest drab-
frequented alley, and her lowest-bowing tradesman, I would
not exchange for Skiddaw, Helvellyn, James, Walter, and
the parson into the bargain. O! her lamps of a night!
her rich goldsmiths, print-shops, toy-shops, mercers,
hardware men, pastry-cooks, St. Paul's Churchyard, the
Strand, Exeter Change, Charing Cross, with the man *upon*
a black horse! These are thy gods, O London! Ain't
you mightily moped on the banks of the Cam? Had you
not better come and set up here? You can't think what
a difference. All the streets and pavements are pure gold,
I warrant you. At least, I know an alchemy that turns
her mud into that metal—a mind that loves to be at home
in crowds."

In a letter to Wordsworth, of somewhat later date, reply-
ing to an invitation to visit the Lakes, he dwells on the
same passionate love for the great city,—the "place of his
kindly engendure"—not alone for its sights and sounds,
its print-shops, and its bookstalls, but for the human faces,
without which the finest scenery failed to satisfy his sense
of beauty. "The wonder of these sights," he says, "im-
pels me into night-walks about her crowded streets, and I

often shed tears in the motley Strand from fulness of joy at so much life. All these emotions must be strange to you; so are your rural emotions to me. But consider what must I have been doing all my life not to have lent great portions of my heart with usury to such scenes?"

"What must I have been doing all my life?" This might well be the language of tender retrospect indulged by some man of sixty. It is that of a young man of six-and-twenty. It serves to show us how much of life had been crowded into those few years.

E

CHAPTER IV.

(1800—1809.)

LAMB was now established in his beloved Temple. For nearly nine years he and his sister resided in Mitre Court Buildings, and for about the same period afterwards within the same sacred precincts, in Inner Temple Lane. Of adventure, domestic or other, his biographer has henceforth little to relate. The track is marked on the one hand by his changes of residence and occasional brief excursions into the country, on the other by the books he wrote and the friendships he formed.

He had written to his friend Manning, as we have seen, how his acquaintance had increased of late. Of such acquaintances Manning himself is the most interesting to us, as having drawn from Lamb a series of letters by far the most important of those belonging to the period before us. Manning was a remarkable person, whose acquaintance Lamb had made on one of his visits to Cambridge during the residence at that University of his friend Lloyd. He was mathematical tutor at Caius, and, in addition to his scientific turn, was possessed by an enthusiasm which in later years he was able to turn to very practical purpose, for exploring the remoter parts of China and Thibet. Lamb had formed a strong admiration for

Manning's genius. He told Crabb Robinson in after
years that he was the most "wonderful man" he had
ever met. Perhaps the circumstance of Manning's two
chief interests in life being so remote from his own, drew
Lamb to him by a kind of "sympathy of difference."
Certainly he made very happy use of the opportunity for
friendly banter thus afforded, and the very absence of a
responsive humour in his correspondent seems to have
imparted an additional richness to his own. Meantime,
to add a few guineas to his scanty income, he was turning
this gift of humour to what end he could. For at least
three years (from 1800 to 1803) he was an occasional contributor of facetious paragraphs, epigrams, and other trifles
to the newspapers of the day. "In those days" as he
afterwards told the world in one of the Elia essays (*Newspapers Thirty-five Years Ago*), "every morning paper, as
an essential retainer to its establishment, kept an author,
who was bound to furnish daily a quantum of witty paragraphs. Sixpence a joke, and it was thought pretty high
too—was Dan Stuart's settled remuneration in these cases.
The chat of the day, scandal, but above all, *dress*, furnished the material. The length of no paragraph was to
exceed seven lines. Shorter they might be, but they
must be poignant." Dan Stuart was editor of the *Morning Post*, and Lamb contributed to this paper, and also to
the *Chronicle* and the *Albion*. Six jokes a day was the
amount he tells us he had to provide during his engagement on the *Post*, and in the essay just cited he dwells
with much humour on the misery of rising two hours
before breakfast (his days being otherwise fully employed
at the India House) to elaborate his jests. " No Egyptian
task-master ever devised a slavery like to that, our
slavery. Half a dozen jests in a day (bating Sundays

E 2

too) why, it seems nothing ; we make twice the number
every day in our lives as a matter of course, and
claim no sabbatical exemptions. But then they come
into our head. But when the head has to go out
to them, when the mountain must go to Mahomet ! "
A few samples of Lamb's work in this line have
been preserved. One political squib has survived, chiefly
perhaps as having served to give the *coup de grace*
to a moribund journal, called the *Albion,* which had been
only a few weeks before purchased (" on tick doubtless,"
Lamb says) by that light-hearted spendthrift, John
Fenwick, immortalized in another of Lamb's essays (*The
Two Races of Men*) as the typical *man who borrows.* The
journal had been in daily expectation of being prosecuted,
when a (not very scathing) epigram of Lamb's on the
apostacy of Sir James Mackintosh, alienated the last of
Fenwick's patrons, Lord Stanhope, and the ' murky
closet,' " late Rackstraw's museum " in Fleet Street, knew
the editor and his contributors no more. Lamb was not
called upon to air his Jacobin principles, survivals from his
old association with Coleridge and Southey, any further in
the newspaper world. " The *Albion* is dead," he writes to
Manning, " dead as nail in door—my revenues have
died with it ; but I am not as a man without hope." He
had got a new introduction, through his old friend George
Dyer, to the *Morning Chronicle,* under the editorship of
Perry. In 1802, we find him again working for the *Post,*
but in a different line. Coleridge was contributing to
that paper, and was doing his best to obtain for Lamb
employment on it of a more dignified character than
providing the daily quantum of jokes. He had proposed
to furnish Lamb with prose versions of German poems for
the latter to turn into metre. Lamb had at first demurred,

on the reasonable ground that Coleridge, whose gift of verse was certainly equal to his own, might as easily do the whole process himself.   But the pressure of pecuniary difficulty was great, and a fortnight later he is telling Coleridge that the experiment shall at least be tried.   " As to the translations, let me do two or three hundred lines, and then do you try the nostrums upon Stuart in any way you please.   If they go down, I will try more.   In fact, if I got, or could but get, fifty pounds a year only, in addition to what I have, I should live in affluence."   By dint of hard work, much against the grain, he contrived during the year that followed to make double the hoped-for sum ; but humour and fancy produced to order could not but fail sooner or later.   It came to an end some time in 1803.   " The best and the worst to me," he writes to Manning in this year (Lamb rarely dates a letter), " is that I have given up two guineas a week at the *Post*, and re-gained my health and spirits, which were upon the wane. I grew sick, and Stuart unsatisfied.   *Ludisti satis, tempus abire est.*   I must cut closer, that's all."

While writing for the newspapers, he had not allowed worthier ambitions to cool.   He was still thinking of success in very different fields.   As early as the year 1799 he had submitted to Coleridge and Southey a five-act drama in blank verse, with the title of *Pride's Cure*, afterwards changed to *John Woodvil.*   His two friends had urgently dissuaded him from publishing, and though he followed this advice, he had not abandoned the hope of seeing it one day upon the stage, and at Christmas of that year had sent it to John Kemble, then manager of Drury Lane.   Nearly a year later, having heard nothing in the meantime from the theatre on the subject, he applied to Kemble to know his fate.   The answer was returned that the manuscript was lost, and Lamb had to furnish a second copy. Later, Kemble went so far as to grant the author a personal interview, but the final result was that the play was declined as unsuitable.

That Lamb should ever have dreamed of any other result may well surprise even those who have some experience of the attitude of a young author to his first drama. *John Woodvil* has no quality that could have made its success on the stage possible. It shows no trace of constructive skill, and the character-drawing is of the crudest. By a strange perverseness of choice, Lamb laid the scene of his drama, written in a language for the most part closely imitated from certain Elizabethan models, in the period of the Restoration, and with a strange carelessness introduced side by side with the imagery and rhythm of Fletcher and Massinger a diction often ludicrously incongruous. Perhaps the most striking feature of the play, regarded as a serious effort, is the entire want of keeping in the dialogue. Certain passages have been often quoted, such as that on which Lamb evidently prided himself most, describing the amusements of the exiled baronet and his son in the forest of Sherwood,—

> To see the sun to bed, and to arise
> Like some hot amourist with glowing eyes,
> Bursting the lazy bands of sleep that bound him
> With all his fires and travelling glories round him.
> *   *   *   *   *
> To view the leaves, thin dancers upon air,
> Go eddying round, and small birds, how they fare,
> When mother autumn fills their beaks with corn
> Filched from the careless Amalthea's horn.

They serve to show how closely Lamb's fancy and his ear were attuned to the music of Shakespeare and

Shakespeare's contemporaries ; but the illusion is suddenly broken by scraps of dialogue sounding the depths of bathos,—

Servant.—Gentlemen, the fireworks are ready.
First Gent.—What be they ?
Lovell.—The work of London artists, which our host has provided in honour of this day.

or by such an image as that with which the play concludes, of the penitent John Woodvil, kneeling on the " hassock " in the " family-pew " of St. Mary Ottery, in the " sweet shire of Devon."

Lamb was not deterred by his failure with the managers from publishing his drama. It appeared in a small duodecimo in 1802 ; and when, sixteen years later, he included it in the first collected edition of his writings, dedicated to Coleridge, he was still able to look with a parent's tenderness upon this child of his early fancy. "When I wrote *John Woodvil*," he says, " Beaumont and Fletcher, and Massinger, were then a *first love,* and from what I was so freshly conversant in, what wonder if my language imperceptibly took a tinge ? " This expresses in fact the real significance of the achievement. Though it is impossible seriously to weigh the merits of *John Woodvil* as a drama, it is yet of interest as the result of the studies of a young man of fine taste and independent judgment in a field of English literature which had lain long unexplored. Within a few years Charles Lamb was to contribute, by more effective methods, to the revived study of the Elizabethan drama, but in the meantime he was doing something, even in *John Woodvil*, to overthrow the despotic conventionalities of eighteenth-century " poetic diction," and to reaccustom the ear to the very different harmonies of an older time.

John Woodvil was noticed in the *Edinburgh Review* for April, 1803. Lamb might have been at that early date too insignificant, personally, to be worth the powder and shot of Jeffrey and his friends, but he was already known as the associate of Coleridge and Southey, and it was this circumstance—as the concluding words of the review rather unguardedly admit—that marked his little volume for the slaughter. He had been already held up to ridicule in the pages of the *Anti-Jacobin*, as sharing the revolutionary sympathies of Coleridge and Southey. It is certainly curious that Lamb, who never "meddled with politics," home or foreign, any more than the *Anti-Jacobin's* knife-grinder himself, should have his name embalmed in that periodical as a leading champion of French Socialism :—

> Coleridge and Southey, Lloyd and Lamb and Co.,
> Tune all your mystic harps to praise Lepeaux.

There was abundant opportunity in Lamb's play for the use of that scourge which the *Edinburgh Review* may be said to have first invented as a critical instrument. Plot and characters, and large portions of the dialogue, lent themselves excellently to the purposes of critical banter, and it was easy to show that Lamb had few qualifications for the task he had undertaken. As he himself observed in his essay on Hogarth : "It is a secret well known to the professors of the art and mystery of criticism, to insist upon what they do not find in a man's works, and to pass over in silence what they do." It was open to the reviewer to note, as even Lamb's friend Southey noted, the "exquisite silliness of the story," but it did not enter into his plan to detect, as Southey had done, the "exquisite beauty" of much of the poetry. The reason why

it is worth while to dwell for a moment on this forgotten
review (not, by the way, by Jeffrey, although Lamb's
friends seem generally to have attributed it to the editor's
own hand) is that it shows how much Lamb was in
advance of his reviewer in familiarity with our older
literature. The review is a piece of pleasantry, of which
it would be absurd to complain, but it is the pleasantry
of an ignorant man. The writer affects to regard the
play as a specimen of the primeval drama. "We have
still among us," he says, "men of the age of Thespis,"
and declares that "the tragedy of Mr. Lamb may indeed
be fairly considered as supplying the first of those lost links
which connect the improvements of Æschylus with the
commencement of the art." Talfourd expresses wonder
that a young critic should "seize on a little eighteen-
penny book, simply printed, without any preface: make
elaborate merriment of its outline, and, giving no hint of
its containing one profound thought or happy expression,
leave the reader of the review at a loss to suggest a motive
for noticing such vapid absurdities." But there is really
little cause for such wonder. The one feature of importance in the little drama is that it here and there imitates
with much skill the imagery and the rhythm of a
family of dramatists whom the world had been content
entirely to forget for nearly two centuries. There is no
reason to suppose that Lamb's reviewer had any acquaintance with these dramatists. The interest of the review
consists in the evidence it affords of a general ignorance,
even among educated men, which Lamb was to do more
than any man of his time to dispel. The passage about
the sports in the Forest, which set William Godwin (who
met with it somewhere as an extract) searching through
Beaumont and Fletcher to find, probably conveyed no idea

whatever, to the Edinburgh Reviewer, save that which
he honestly confessed, that here was a specimen of versification which had been long ago improved from off the
face of the earth.

In the summer of 1802 Charles and his sister spent
their holiday, three weeks, with Coleridge at Keswick.
The letters to Coleridge and Manning referring to this
visit show pleasantly that there was something of affectation in the disparaging tone with which Charles was wont
to speak of the charms of scenery. Though on occasion
he would make his friends smile by telling that when he
ascended Skiddaw he was obliged, in self-defence, to revert
in memory to the ham-and-beef shop in St. Martin's Lane,
it is evident from his enthusiastic words to Manning
that the Lake scenery had moved and delighted him.
" Coleridge dwells," he writes to Manning, " upon a
small hill by the side of Keswick, in a comfortable house,
quite enveloped on all sides by a net of mountains : great
floundering bears and monsters they seemed, all couchant
and asleep. We got in in the evening, travelling in a
post-chaise from Penrith, in the midst of a gorgeous sun-
set which transmuted all the mountains into colours,
purple, &c. &c. We thought we had got into Fairyland.
But that went off (as it never came again, while we stayed
we had no more fine sunsets) ; and we entered Coleridge's
comfortable study just in the dusk, when the mountains
were all dark with clouds upon their heads. Such an
impression I never received from objects of sight before,
nor do I suppose that I can ever again. Glorious creatures,
fine old fellows, Skiddaw, &c., I never shall forget ye,
how ye lay about that night, like an entrenchment ; gone
to bed, as it seemed for the night, but promising that ye
were to be seen in the morning." And later, " We have

clambered up to the top of Skiddaw, and I have waded
up the bed of Lodore. In fine, I have satisfied myself
that there is such a thing as that which tourists call
romantic, which I very much suspected before." And
again, of Skiddaw, " Oh, its fine black head, and the bleak
air atop of it, with a prospect of mountains all about and
about, making you giddy ; and then Scotland afar off, and
the border countries so famous in song and ballad ! It
was a day that will stand out like a mountain, I am sure,
in my life."

It is pleasant to read of these intervals of bracing air,
both to body and mind, in the story of the brother and sister,
for the picture of the home life in the Temple lodging at
this time, drawn by the same frank hand, is anything but
cheerful. This very letter to Manning (who was apparently spending his holiday in Switzerland) goes on to hint
of grave anxieties and responsibilities belonging to the life
in London. " My habits are changing, I think, i. e. from
drunk to sober. Whether I shall be happier or not
remains to be proved. I shall certainly be more happy
in a morning ; but whether I shall not sacrifice the fat,
and the marrow, and the kidneys—i. e. the night, glorious
care-drowning night, that heals all our wrongs, pours wine
into our mortifications, changes the scene from indifferent
and flat to bright and brilliant ? O Manning, if I should
have formed a diabolical resolution by the time you come
to England, of not admitting any spirituous liquors into
my house, will you be my guest on such shameworthy
terms ? Is life, with such limitations, worth trying ?
The truth is that my liquors bring a nest of friendly
harpies about my house, who consume me. This is a pitiful
tale to be read at St. Gothard, but it is just now nearest
my heart."

The tale is indeed a sad one, and we have no reason to
suppose it less true than pitiful. There is no concealment
on the part of Lamb himself, or his sister, or of those who
knew him most intimately, of the fact that from an early
age Charles found in wine, or its equivalents, a stimulus
that relieved him under the pressure of shyness, anxiety,
and low spirits, and that the habit remained with him till
the end of his life. It is not easy to deal with this
"frailty" (to borrow Talfourd's expression) in Lamb,
without falling into an apologetic tone, suggestive of the
much-abused proverb connecting excuse with accusation.
But it is the biographer's task to account for these things,
if not to excuse them, and at this period there is not
wanting evidence of hard trials attending the life of the
brother and sister which may well prompt a treatment
of the subject, the reverse of harsh. There is a correspondence extant of Mary Lamb with Miss Stoddart, who
afterwards became the wife of William Hazlitt, which
throws much sad light on the history of the joint home
during these years. The pressure of poverty was being
keenly felt. "I hope, when I write next," she says, early
in 1804, "I shall be able to tell you Charles has begun
something which will produce a little money : for it is not
well to be *very poor*, which we certainly are at this present
writing." Charles' engagement as contributor of squibs
and occasional paragraphs to the *Morning Post* had come to
an end, just before this letter of Mary's : but poverty was
not the worst of the home troubles. It is too clear that
both brother and sister suffered from constant and haras-
sing depression, and that their heroic determination to
live entirely for each other, only made matters worse.
"It has been sad and heavy times with us lately," Mary
writes in the year following (1805). "When I am pretty

well, his low spirits throw me back again ; and when he begins to get a little cheerful, then I do the same kind office for him ;" and again, " Do not say anything when you write, of our low spirits—it will vex Charles. You would laugh, or you would cry, perhaps both, to see us sit together, looking at each other with long and rueful faces, and saying ' How do you do ?   and ' How do you do ?' and then we fall a crying, and say we will be better on the morrow. He says we are like toothache and his friend gum-boil, which though a kind of ease, is but an uneasy kind of ease, a comfort of rather an uncomfortable sort." In the following year we gather that Charles, still bent on success in the drama as the most likely means of adding to his income, had begun to write a farce, and finding the gloom here described intolerable, in such an association, had taken a cheap lodging hard by to which he might retire, and pursue his work without distraction. But the more utter solitude proved as intolerable as the depressing influences of home. " The lodging," writes Mary Lamb, " is given up, and *here he is again*—Charles, I mean—as unsettled and as undetermined as ever. When he went to the poor lodging, after the holidays I told you he had taken, he could not endure the solitariness of them, and I had no rest for the sole of my foot till I promised to believe his solemn protestations that he could and would write as well at home as there."

There is a remark in this same letter, hardly more touching than it is indicative of the clear-sighted wisdom of this true-hearted woman. " Our love for each other," she writes, " has been the torment of our lives hitherto. I am most seriously intending to bend the whole force of my mind to counteract this, and I think I see some prospect of success." It doubtless was this strong affection, working by ill-considered means, that made much of the unhappiness of Charles Lamb's life. His sense of what he owed to his sister, who had been mother and sister in one, his admiration for her character, and his profound pity for her affliction, made him resolve that no other tie, no other taste or pleasure, should interfere with the prime duty of cleaving to her as long as life should last. But this exclusive devotion was not a good thing for either. They wanted some strong human interests from outside to assist them to bear those of home. They were both fond of society. In their later more prosperous days they saw much society of a brilliant and notable sort, but already Charles had made the discovery that "open house" involved temptation of a kind he had not learnt to resist. The little suppers, at home and with friends elsewhere, meant too much punch and too much tobacco, and the inevitable sequel of depression and moroseness on the morrow. "He came home very *smoky and drinky* last night," is the frequent burden of Miss Lamb's letters. And so it came to pass that his social life was spent too much between these two extremes —the companionship of that one sister, anxiety for whose health was always pressing, and whose inherited instincts were too like his own, and the convivialities which banished melancholy for a while and set his fancy and his speech at liberty, but too often did *not* bear the morning's reflection. He needed at this time fewer companions, but more friends. Coleridge, Southey, Wordsworth, Manning, were all out of London, and only in his scanty holidays, or on occasion of their rare visits to town, could he take counsel with them.

One pleasant gleam of sunshine among the driving clouds of those years of anxiety is afforded in the lines

on Hester Savary. During the few months that Lamb
and his sister lodged at Pentonville in 1800, he had
fallen in love (for the second and last time) with a young
Quakeress. In sending the verses to Manning (in Paris)
in 1803, Lamb recalls the old attachment as one his
friend would remember having heard him mention.
However ardent it may have been, it was presumably without hope of requital, for Lamb admits that he had never
spoken to the lady in his life. He may have met her
daily in his walks to and from the office, or have watched
her week by week on her way to that Quaker's meeting
he has so lovingly described elsewhere. And now, only
a month before, she had died, and Lamb's true vein,
unspoiled by squibs and paragraphs written to order for
party journals, flows once more in its native purity and
sweetness :—

> When maidens such as Hester die
> Their place ye may not well supply,
> Though ye among a thousand try
>   With vain endeavour.
> A month or more hath she been dead,
> Yet cannot I by force be led
> To think upon the wormy bed
>   And her together.
>
> A springy motion in her gait,
> A rising step, did indicate
> Of pride and joy no common rate
>   That flushed her spirit.
> I know not by what name beside
> I shall it call : if 'twas not pride,
> It was a joy to that allied
>   She did inherit.
>
> Her parents held the Quaker rule
> Which doth the human spirit cool :

> But she was trained in Nature's school,
>   Nature had blest her.
> A waking eye, a prying mind,
> A heart that stirs, is hard to bind :
> A hawk's keen sight ye cannot blind,—
>   Ye could not Hester.
>
> My sprightly neighbour, gone before
> To that unknown and silent shore,
> Shall we not meet, as heretofore,
>   Some summer morning—
> When from thy cheerful eyes a ray
> Hath struck a bliss upon the day,
> A bliss that would not go away,
>   A sweet fore-warning ?

These charming verses are themselves a "sweet fore-warning" of happier times to come. New friends were at hand, and new interests in literature were soon to bring a little cheerful relief to the monotony of the Temple lodging. We have already heard something of a play in preparation. The first intimation of Lamb's resolve to tempt dramatic fortune once again is in a letter to Wordsworth, in September, 1805. "I have done nothing," he writes, "since the beginning of last year, when I lost my newspaper job, and having had a long idleness, I must do something, or we shall get very poor. Sometimes I think of a farce, but hitherto all schemes have gone off; an idle brag or two of an evening, vapouring out of a pipe, and going off in the morning; but now I have bid farewell to my 'sweet enemy' tobacco, as you will see in the next page, I shall perhaps set nobly to work. Hang work!" He did set to work, in good heart, during the six months that followed. Mary Lamb's letters contain frequent references to the farce in progress, and before Midsummer, 1806, it was completed, and accepted by the proprietors of Drury Lane. The farce was the celebrated *Mr. H.*

No episode of Lamb's history is better known than the production, and the summary failure of this *jeu d'esprit*. That it failed is no matter for surprise, and most certainly none for regret. Though it had the advantage, in its leading character, of the talent of Elliston, the best light-comedian of his day, the slightness of the interest (dealing with the inconveniences befalling a gentleman who is ashamed to confess that his real name is Hogsflesh) was too patent for the best acting to contend against. Crabb Robinson, one of Lamb's more recent friends, accompanied the brother and sister to the first and only performance, and received the impression that the audience resented the vulgarity of the name, when it was at last revealed, rather than the flimsiness of the plot. But the latter is quite sufficient to account for what happened. The curtain fell amid a storm of hisses, in which Lamb is said to have taken a conspicuous share. Indeed, his genuine critical faculty must have come to his deliverance when he thus viewed his own work from the position of an outsider. He expresses no surprise at the result, after the first few utterances of natural disappoin   n ⟨⟩ mortification must have been considerable. The brother and sister had looked forward to a success. They sorely needed the money it might have brought them, and Charles' deep-seated love of all things dramatic made success in that field a much cherished hope. But he bore his failure, as he bore all his disappointments in life, with a cheerful sweetness. He writes to Hazlitt : " Mary is a little cut at the ill-success of *Mr. H.*, which came out last night and *failed*. I know you'll be sorry, but never mind. We are determined not to be cast down. I am going to leave off tobacco, and then we must thrive. A smoky man must write smoky farces." It must be

F

admitted that *Mr. H.* is not much better in reading than
it was found in the acting. Its humour, consisting
largely of puns and other verbal pleasantries, exhibits little
or nothing of Lamb's native vein, and the dialogue is too
often laboriously imitated from the conventional comedy-
dialogue then in vogue. But even had this been different,
the lack of constructive ability already shown in *John
Woodvil* must have made success as a writer for the stage
quite beyond his reach.

He was on safer ground, though not perhaps working so
thoroughly *con amore*, in another literary enterprise of
this time. In 1805, he had made the acquaintance of
William Hazlitt, and Hazlitt had introduced him to
William Godwin. Godwin had started, as his latest
venture, a series of books for children, to which he himself
contributed under the name of Edward Baldwin. Lamb,
writing to his friend Manning, in May, 1806, thus
describes a joint task in which he and his sister were
engaged in connexion with this scheme : " She is doing
for Godwin's bookseller twenty of Shakespeare's plays, to
be made into children's tales. Six are already done by
her, to wit, *The Tempest, Winter's Tale, Midsummer
Night, Much Ado, Two Gentlemen of Verona,* and *Cym-
beline;* and the *Merchant of Venice* is in forwardness. I
have done *Othello* and *Macbeth*, and mean to do all the
tragedies. I think it will be popular among the little
people, besides money. It's to bring in sixty guineas.
Mary has done them capitally, I think you'd think." Mary
herself supplements this account in a way that makes
curiously vivid to us the homely realities of their joint
life. She writes about the same time : " Charles has
written *Macbeth, Othello, King Lear*, and has begun
Hamlet. You would like to see us, as we often sit writing

on one table (but not on one cushion sitting), like *Hermia*
and *Helena*, in the *Midsummer Night's Dream ;* or rather
like an old literary Darby and Joan, I taking snuff, and he
groaning all the while, and saying he can make nothing of
it, which he always says till he has finished, and then he
finds out he has made something of it." Writing these
Tales from Shakespeare was no doubt task-work to the
brother and sister, but it was task-work on a congenial
theme, and one for which they had special qualifications.
They had, to start with, a profound and intimate acquaintance with their original, which set them at an infinite distance from the usual compilers of such books for children.
They had, moreover, command of a style, Wordsworthian
in its simplicity and purity, that enabled them to write
down to the level of a child's understanding, without any
appearance of condescension. The very homeliness of the
style may easily divert attention from the rare critical
faculty, the fine analysis of character, that marks the
writers' treatment of the several plays. It is no wonder
that the publisher in announcing a subsequent edition
was able to boast that a book designed for young children
had been found suitable for those of more advanced age.
There is, indeed, no better introduction to the study of
Shakespeare than these *Tales*—no better initiation into
the mind of Shakespeare, and into the subtleties of his
language and rhythm. For the ear of both Charles and
Mary Lamb had been trained on the cadences of Elizabethan English, and they were able throughout to weave
the very words of Shakespeare into their narrative without
producing any effect of discrepancy between the old and
the new.

The *Tales* were published in 1807, and were a success,
a second edition appearing in the following year. One

result of this success was a commission from Godwin to
make another version of a great classic for the benefit of
children, the story of the *Odyssey*. Lamb was no Greek
scholar, but he had been, like Keats, stirred by the rough
vigour of Chapman's translation. "Chapman is divine,"
he said afterwards to Bernard Barton, "and my abridg-
ment has not quite emptied him of his divinity." And
the few words of preface with which he modestly introduced his little book as a supplement to that well-known
school classic the *Adventures of Telemachus*, shows that the
moral value of this record of human vicissitude had moved
him not less than the variety of the adventure. "The
picture which he exhibits," he writes, "is that of a brave
man struggling with adversity; by a wise use of events,
and with an inimitable presence of mind under difficulties,
forcing out a way for himself through the severest trials to
which human life can be exposed; with enemies natural
and supernatural surrounding him on all sides. The
agents in this tale, besides men and women, are giants,
enchanters, sirens; things which denote external force or
internal temptations, the two-fold danger which a wise
fortitude must expect to encounter in its course through
this world." We cannot be wrong in judging that Charles
Lamb had seen in this "wisdom of the ancients" an
image of sirens and enchanters, of trials and disciplines, that
beset the lonely dweller at home not less surely than the
wanderer from city to city, and had found therein something of a cordial and a tonic for himself. No one felt
more repugnance than did Lamb to the appending of a
formal moral to a work of art, to use his own comparison,
like the " God send the good ship safe into harbour " at
the end of a bill of lading. But it was to be his special
note as a critic that he could not keep his human com-

passion from blending with his judgment of every work of human imagination. If his strength as a critic was—and remains for us—as the "strength of ten," it was because his heart was pure.

To what masterly purpose he had been long training this faculty of criticism he was now about to show. The letter to Manning, which tells of his *Adventures of Ulysses*, announces a more important undertaking— apparently a commission from the firm of Longman— *Specimens of English Dramatic Poets contemporary with Shakespeare.* " Specimens," he writes, " are becoming fashionable. We have *Specimens of Ancient English Poets, Specimens of Modern English Poets, Specimens of Ancient English Prose Writers*, without end. They used to be called ' Beauties.' You have seen *Beauties of Shakespeare ?* so have many people that never saw any beauties *in* Shakespeare." But Lamb's method was to have little in common with that of the unfortunate Dr. Dodd. " It is to have notes," is the brief mention of that feature of the collection which was at once to place their author in the first rank of critics. The commentary, often extending to no more than a dozen or twenty lines appended to each scene, or each author chosen for illustration, was of a kind new to a generation accustomed to the *Variorum* school of annotator. It contains no philology, no antiquarianism, no discussion of difficult or corrupt passages. It takes its character from the principle set forth in the Preface on which the selection of scenes is made :—

The kind of extracts which I have sought after have been, not so much passages of wit and humour—though the old plays are rich in such—as scenes of passion, sometimes of the deepest quality, interesting situations, serious descriptions, that which is more nearly allied to poetry than to wit, and to tragic rather

than comic poetry. The plays which I have made choice of have
been with few exceptions those which treat of human life and
manners, rather than masques and Arcadian Pastorals, with
their train of abstractions, unimpassioned deities, passionate
mortals, Claius, and Medorus, and Amintas, and Amaryllis. My
leading design has been to illustrate what may be called the
moral sense of our ancestors. To show in what manner they
felt when they placed themselves by the power of imagination
in trying situations, in the conflicts of duty and passion, or the
strife of contending duties ; what sort of loves and enmities
theirs were ; how their griefs were tempered, and their full-
swoln joys abated ; how much of Shakespeare shines in the great
men his contemporaries, and how far in his divine mind and
manners he surpassed them and all mankind.

The very idea of the collection was a bold one. When
we cast our eye over the list of now familiar names, Marlowe and Peele, Marston, Chapman, Ford, and Webster,
from whom Lamb chose his scenes, we must not forget
that he was pleading their merits before a public which
knew them only as names, if it knew them at all. With
the one exception of Shakespeare, the dramatists of the
period, between " the middle of Elizabeth's reign and the
close of the reign of Charles I.," were unknown to the
general reader of the year 1808. Shakespeare, indeed,
had a permanent stage-existence—that best of commen-
taries which fine acting supplies, to which Lamb himself
had been from childhood so largely indebted. But for
those who studied him in the closet there was no aid to
his interpretation save such as was supplied by the very
unilluminating notes of Johnson or Malone. And this
circumstance must be taken into account if we would
rightly estimate the genius of Lamb. As a critic he had
no master—it might almost be said, no predecessor. He
was the inventor of his own art. As the friend of Cole-

ridge, he might have heard something of that school of dramatic criticism of which Lessing was the founder, but there is little trace of any such influence in Lamb's own critical method. And though, three years later, Coleridge was to make another contribution of value to the same cause, in the Lectures on Shakespeare delivered at the London Philosophical Society, it is likely that his obligations were at least as great to Lamb, as those of Lamb had ever been, in the same field, to Coleridge.

The suggestion in the preface, already cited, of Shakespeare as the representative dramatist, the standard by which his contemporaries must be content to be judged, is amply followed up in the notes, and gives a unity of its own to a collection so miscellaneous. I may refer, as examples, to the masterly distinction drawn between the use made of the supernatural by Middleton in the *Witch*, and by Shakespeare in *Macbeth*, and again to the contrast indicated between the Dirge in Webster's *White Devil* and the "Ditty which reminds Ferdinand of his drowned father in the *Tempest*"—"as that is of the water, watery; so is this of the earth, earthy. Both have that intenseness of feeling which seems to resolve itself into the elements which it contemplates,"—a criticism which could only have been conceived by one who was himself a poet. How admirably again does he draw attention (in a note on the *Merry Devil of Edmonton*) to that feature of Shakespeare's genius which perhaps more than any other is forced upon the reader's mind as he turns from passage to passage in this collection :—"This scene has much of Shakespeare's manner in the sweetness and good-naturedness of it. It seems written to make the reader happy. Few of our dramatists or novelists have attended enough to this. They torture and wound us abundantly. They are

economists only in delight." Nothing, again, can be
more profound than his remark on the elaborate and
ostentatious saintliness of Ordella (in Fletcher's *Thierry
and Theodoret*). "Shakespeare had nothing of this con-
tortion in his mind, none of that craving after romantic
incidents, and flights of strained and improbable virtue,
which I think always betray an imperfect moral sensibility."
And yet though Lamb's fine judgment approved the
fidelity to nature, and the artistic self-control, which he
here emphasises in his great model, it is clear that the
audacious conceptions, both of character and situation, in
which writers such as Ford and Tourneur indulged, had
no small fascination for him. As he recalled the dreary
types of virtue, the "insipid levelling morality to which
the modern stage is tied down," he turned with joy—as
from a heated saloon into the fresh air—to the "vigorous
passions" the "virtues clad in flesh and blood," with
which the old dramatists presented him. And this joy in
the presentment of the naked human soul is felt throughout all his criticisms on the more terrible scenes of Shakespeare's successors. His "ears tingle," or his eyes fill, or
his heart leaps within him, as Calantha dies of her Broken
Heart, or Webster's Duchess yields slowly to the torture.
Hence it is that Lamb's criticism as often takes the form
of a study of human life, as of the dramatist's art. And
hence also the effect he often leaves of having indulged in
praise too great for the occasion. There is, moreover,
another reason for this last-named result, which was inseparable from Lamb's method. No two dramatists can be
measured by comparing passage with passage, scene with
scene. Shakespeare and Marlowe cannot be compared or
contrasted by setting the death of Edward II. side by side
with that of Richard II. Drama must be put side by side

with drama. Lamb does not indeed suggest, by anything that he says, that the rank of a dramatist can be decided by passages or extracts. Only it did not enter into his scheme to dwell upon that supreme art of construction, and that highest gift of characterization, which are needed to make the perfect dramatist. In "profoundness of single thoughts," in "richness of imagery," in "abundance of illustration," he could produce passage after passage from Shakespeare's contemporaries that evinced genius nearly allied to Shakespeare's; but of that "fundamental excellence" which "distinguishes the artist from the mere amateur, that power of execution which creates, forms, and constitutes," it was not possible for him to supply example. And this reservation the student must be prepared to make, who would approach the study of the Elizabethan Drama by the aid of Charles Lamb's specimens.

But, whatever qualification must be interposed, it is certain that the publication of these extracts, and the accompanying commentary, has a well-defined place in the poetical renascence that marked the early years of this century. The revived study of the old English dramatists—other than Shakespeare—dates from this publication. Coleridge had not yet begun to lecture, nor Hazlitt to write, and it was not till some twenty years later that Mr. Dyce began his different, but not less important, labours in the same field. To Lamb must be allowed the credit of having first recalled attention to a range of poetical excellence, in forgetfulness of which English poetry had too long pined and starved. It was to these mountain-heights of inspiration—not to the cultivated lowlands of the eighteenth century—that poetry was to turn her eyes for help.

CHAPTER V.

TALFOURD made the acquaintance of Charles Lamb early
in the year 1815, and has recorded the impression left
by his appearance and manner at that time in words
which at this stage of our memoir it may be convenient to quote. Lamb has been fortunate in his
verbal describers, if not in the attempts of the painter's
art to convey a true idea of his outward man. Leigh
Hunt has declared that " there never was a true portrait
of Lamb "—and those who take the trouble to examine in
succession the half-dozen portraits that are in existence
are obliged to admit that it is difficult to derive from them
any consistent idea of his features and expression. But it
so happens that we have full length portraits of him drawn
by other hands, which more than compensate for this
want. Poets, critics, and humourists, of kindred genius,
have left on record how Charles Lamb appeared to them ;
and though the various accounts bear, as might be expected, the strong impress of their writers' individuality,
and though each naturally gives most prominence to
the traits that struck him most, the final impression
left is one of agreement, in remarkable degree. We have
descriptions of Lamb, all possessing points of great

interest by Talfourd, Procter, Hood, Patmore, and others, and from these it is possible to learn how their subject looked and spoke and bore himself, with a precision and vividness that we are seldom in such cases allowed to enjoy. I have the advantage of being able to confirm their accounts by the testimony of a living witness. Mr. James Crossley, of Manchester, has related to me his recollections of more than one interview which he had with Lamb, nearly sixty years ago, and has kindly allowed me to make use of them.

Talfourd's reminiscence, committed to writing shortly after Lamb's death, if slightly idealized by his own poetic temperament, is not for that reason a less satisfactory basis on which to form a conception of Charles Lamb's appearance. "Methinks I see him before me now, as he appeared then, and as he continued with scarcely any perceptible alteration to me, during the twenty years of intimacy which followed, and were closed by his death. A light frame, so fragile that it seemed as if a breath would overthrow it, clad in clerk-like black, was surmounted by a head of form and expression the most noble and sweet. His black hair curled crisply about an expanded forehead; his eyes, softly brown, twinkled with varying expression, though the prevalent feeling was sad; and the nose slightly curved, and delicately carved at the nostril, with the lower outline of the face regularly oval, completed a head which was finely placed on the shoulders, and gave importance and even dignity to a diminutive and shadowy stem. Who shall describe his countenance, catch its quivering sweetness, and fix it for ever in words? There are none, alas, to answer the vain desire of friendship. Deep thought, striving with humour; the lines of suffering wreathed into cordial mirth; and a smile of painful

sweetness, present an image to the mind it can as little
describe as lose. His personal appearance and manner
are not unfitly characterized by what he himself says in
one of his letters to Manning, of Braham, 'a compound
of the Jew, the gentleman, and the angel.' "

From this tender and charming sketch it is instructive
to turn to the rude etching on copper made by Mr. Brook
Pulham from life, in the year 1825, which in the opinion
of Lamb's biographers (and Mr. Crossley confirms their
judgment) gives a better idea than all other existing portraits, of Charles Lamb's outward man. The small stature
—he was very noticeably below the middle height—the
head apparently out of proportion to the slender frame,
the Jewish cast of nose, the long black hair, the figure
dwindling away down to "almost immaterial legs," the
tight-fitting clerk-like suit of black, terminating in gaiters
and straps, all these appear in Mr. Pulham's etching in
such bold realism that the portrait might easily pass for
a caricature, were it not confirmed in all its details
by other authorities. Mr. Crossley recalls with perfect
distinctness the aspect of Lamb as he sat at his desk in
his room at the India House, looking the more diminutive
for being perched upon a very high stool. His hair and
complexion were so dark, that when looked at in combination with the complete suit of solemn black, they suggested
old Fuller's description of the negro, of which Lamb
was so fond—an image "cut in ebony." He might have
passed, Hood tells us, for a "Quaker in black." "He
had a long melancholy face," says Mr. Procter, "with
keen penetrating eyes." "There was altogether," Mr.
Patmore says, "a Rabbinical look about Lamb's head
which was at once striking and impressive." But the
feature of his expression that all his friends dwell on

with most loving emphasis is "the bland sweet smile,
with the touch of sadness in it;" and Mr. Patmore's
description of the general impression produced by
this countenance well sums up and confirms the testimony of all other friends : "In point of intellectual
character and expression, a finer face was never seen, nor
one more fully, however vaguely corresponding with the
mind whose features it interpreted.   There was the gravity
usually engendered by a life passed in book learning,
without the slightest tinge of that assumption and affectation which almost always attend the gravity so engendered ; the intensity and elevation of general expression
that mark high genius, without any of its pretension and
its oddity ; the sadness waiting on fruitless thoughts and
baffled aspirations, but no evidence of that spirit of scorn-
ing and contempt which these are apt to engender.   Above
all there was a pervading sweetness and gentleness which
went straight to the heart of every one who looked on it :
and not the less so, perhaps, that it bore about it an air, a
something, seeming to tell that it was—not *put on*—for
nothing would be more unjust than to tax Lamb with
assuming anything, even a virtue, which he did not possess
—but preserved and persevered in, spite of opposing and
contradictory feelings within that struggled in vain for
mastery.   It was a thing to remind you of that painful
smile which bodily disease and agony will sometimes put
on, to conceal their sufferings from the observation of those
they love."

We know Charles Lamb's history, and have not to ask
for any explanation of the appearances thus described.   He
had always (it must not be forgotten) to contend against
sad memories, and anticipations of further sorrow.   He was
by nature" terribly shy," and his difficulties of speech, and

possibly a consciousness of oddity of manner and appearance, aggravated this diffidence. It was " terrible " to him
—as he confessed to Mr. Procter one morning when they
were going together to breakfast with Rogers—to undergo
the scrutiny of servants. Hence only at times, and in certain
companies, was he entirely at his ease ; and it is evident
that when in the society of those in sympathy with him
and his tastes, he conveyed an entirely different impression
of himself from that left under the opposite circumstances.
Before strangers, or uncongenial acquaintance, he was uncomfortable, and if not actually silent, generally indulged
in some line of conversation or vein of sentiment foreign
to his own real nature. Like most men, Charles Lamb
had various oddnesses, contradictions, perverseness of
temper, and unless he was in company of those who
loved him (and who he *knew* loved him), and understood him, he was very prone, in a spirit of what
children call " contrariness," to set to work to alienate
them still more from any possibility of sympathy with
him. Something of this must of course be laid to
the account of the extra glass of wine or spirits that so
often determined his mood for the evening, only that when
Procter, or Talfourd, or Coleridge, or Hazlitt were round
his hospitable table, this stimulus served but to set free
the richer and more generous springs of thought and fancy
within him. I have the authority of Mr. Crossley for
saying that on one evening when in manner, speech, and
walk, Lamb was obviously under the influence of what he
had drunk, he discoursed at length upon Milton, with a
fulness of knowledge, an eloquence, and a profundity
of critical power, which left an impression upon Mr.
Crossley, never to be effaced. But we know that the
wine was not in this case the good, any more than on

other occasions it was the evil, influence. "It *created* nothing," says Mr. Patmore, "but it was the talisman that not only unlocked the poor casket in which the rich thoughts of Charles Lamb were shut up, but set in motion that machinery in the absence of which they would have lain like gems in the mountain or gold in the mine." But where the society was unsympathetic, the wine often set free less lovable springs of fancy in Charles Lamb. He would take up a perverse attitude of contradiction, with too slight regard for the courtesies of human intercourse, or else give play to a mere spirit of reckless and not very edifying mockery. The same enthusiastic friend and admirer just quoted is obliged to admit that " to those who did not know him, or knowing, did not and could not appreciate him, Lamb often passed for something between an imbecile, a brute, and a buffoon ; and the first impression he made on ordinary people was always un-favourable, sometimes to a violent and repulsive degree." Many persons have of late been startled by the discovery that Lamb sometimes left the same impression upon people the reverse of ordinary.   Nothing perhaps in the Reminis-cences of Thomas Carlyle has provoked so much surprise, and hurt so many feelings, as his passing criticism upon Lamb.   And yet it is entirely supported and explained by Mr. Patmore's observation.   No two persons could have been more antipathetic than Lamb and Carlyle, and nothing therefore is less surprising than that to the author of the *Latter-Day Pamphlets* Charles and his sister should have appeared two very " sorry phenomena," or that the scraps of Lamb's talk which he overheard during a pass-ing call should often have seemed " contemptibly small," " ghastly make-believe of wit," and the rest.   There is no need to question the substantial justice of this report.   It is only too probable that the presence of the austere and dyspeptic Scotchman (one of that nation Lamb had all his days been trying in vain to like) made him more than usually disposed to roduce his entire stock of frivolity. He had a perverse delight in shocking uncongenial society. Another noticeable person—very different in all respects from Carlyle—has left a record, significant by its very brevity, of his single interview with Lamb. Macready tells in his diary how he was asked to meet him at Talfourd's, and this is what he records of the interview : " I noted one odd saying of Lamb's, that ' the last breath he drew in he wished might be through a pipe, and exhaled in a pun.' " Lamb may have discovered at a glance that he and the great tragedian were not likely to take the same views of men and things. Perhaps his love both for joking and smoking had struck Macready the reverse of favourably, and if so, it was quite in Lamb's way to clench once for all the unfavourable impression by such an " odd saying " as that just quoted.

Charles Lamb has drawn for us a character of himself, but, so fond was he of hoaxes and mystifications of this kind, that we might have hesitated to accept it as faithful, were it not in such precise accord with the testimony of others already cited. The second series of the *Essays of Elia* was introduced by a Preface, purporting to be written " by a friend of the late Elia," but of course from Charles's own hand. In this preface he assumes Elia to have actually died, and after some preliminary remarks on his writings thus proceeds to describe his character and manners :—

My late friend was in many respects a singular character. Those who did not like him, hated him ; and some, who once liked him, afterwards became his bitterest haters. The truth is, he gave himself too little concern what he uttered, and in

whose presence. He observed neither time nor place, and
would e'en out with what came uppermost. With the severe
religionist he would pass for a free-thinker; while the other
faction set him down for a bigot, or persuaded themselves that
he belied his sentiments. Few understood him, and I am not
certain that at all times he quite understood himself. He too
much affected that dangerous figure—irony. He sowed doubt-
ful speeches, and reaped plain, unequivocal hatred. He would
interrupt the gravest discussion with some light jest; and yet,
perhaps, not quite irrelevant in ears that could understand it.
Your long and much talkers hated him. The informal habit of
his mind, joined to an inveterate impediment of speech, forbade
him to be an orator; and he seemed determined that no one else
should play that part when he was present. He was *petit* and
ordinary in his person and appearance. I have seen him sometimes in what is called good company, but where he has been a
stranger, sit silent and be suspected for an odd fellow; till some
unlucky occasion provoking it, he would stutter out some senseless pun (not altogether senseless, perhaps, if rightly taken)
which has stamped his character for the evening. It was hit or
miss with him; but nine times out of ten he contrived by this
device to send away a whole company his enemies. His conceptions rose kindlier than his utterance, and his happiest *im-
promptus* had the appearance of effort. He has been accused of
trying to be witty, when in truth he was but struggling to give
his poor thoughts articulation. He chose his companions for
some individuality of character which they manifested. Hence
not many persons of science, and few professed *literati*, were of
his councils. They were, for the most part, persons of an uncertain fortune; and as to such people commonly nothing is
more obnoxious than a gentleman of settled (though moderate)
income, he passed with most of them for a great miser. To my
knowledge this was a mistake. His *intimados*, to confess a truth
were in the world's eye a ragged regiment. He found them
floating on the surface of society; and the colour, or something
else, in the weed pleased him. The burrs stuck to him; but
they were good and loving burrs for all that. He never greatly

cared for the society of what are called good people. If any of
these were scandalized (and offences were sure to arise) he could
not help it. When he has been remonstrated with for not
making more concessions to the feelings of good people, he
would retort by asking what one point did these good people
ever concede to him? He was temperate in his meals and
diversions, but always kept a little on this side of abstemious-
ness. Only in the use of the Indian weed he might be thought
a little excessive. He took it, he would say, as a solvent
of speech. Marry—as the friendly vapour ascended, how his
prattle would curl up sometimes with it! the ligaments which
tongue-tied him were loosened, and the stammerer proceeded a
statist !

When a man's account of himself—his foibles and
eccentricities—is confirmed in minutest detail by those
who knew and loved him best, it is reasonable to conclude
that we are not far wrong in accepting it, and this self-
portraiture of Lamb's gives an unexpected plausibility to
the judgments, which otherwise have a harsh sound, of
Mr. Patmore and Carlyle. The peculiarities which Lamb
here enumerates are just those which are little likely
ever to receive gentle consideration from the world.

Lamb's mention of the "senseless pun" which often
"stamped his character for the evening," suggests oppor-
tunely the subject of his reputation as a humourist and
wit. This habit of playing upon words was a part of
him through life, and as in the case of most who indulge
in it, became an outlet for whatever mood was for the
moment dominant in Charles Lamb's mind. When he
was ill at ease, and in an attitude (as he often was) of
antagonism to his company, it would take the shape of a
wanton interruption of the argument under discussion.
To use a simile of Mr. Oliver Wendell Holmes, it was the
halfpenny laid upon the line by a mischievous boy to

upset a whole train of cars. When he was annoyed, he
made annoying puns, — when he was frivolous, he made
frivolous puns, but when he was in the cue, and his
surroundings were such as to call forth his better powers,
he put into this form of wit, humour and imagination of
a high order. Samples of all these kinds have been preserved, and are not without use as showing the various
moods of his many-sided nature, but it is pitiable to read
long strings of them, set down without any discrimination,
and to be asked to accept them as specimens of Lamb's
" wit and humour." Many of his jests thus handed down
are little more than amusing evidence of a restless levity,
and almost petulant impatience of the restraints of serious
discourse. Much of his conversational humour took the
form of retort—courteous, or the reverse. Sometimes these
embodied a criticism so luminous or acute that they have
survived, not only for their drollery, or even their severity.
" Charles, did you ever hear me preach ? " asked Coleridge,
referring to the days of his Unitarian ministry. " I never
heard you do anything else," was the reply. When
Wordsworth was discussing with him the degree of
originality to be allowed to Shakespeare, as borrowing
his plots from sources ready to his hand, and was even
hinting that other poets, with the *History of Hamblet* before them, might have been equally successful in adapting
it to the stage, Charles cried out, " Oh ! here's Wordsworth
says he could have written *Hamlet*, if *he'd had the mind*."
In both these cases the retort embodies a felicitous judgment. A foible—if in either case it is to be called a foible—
in the character of the two poets, respectively, flashes out
into sudden light. The pun is more than a pun ; the wit
is more than wit ; it is a sudden glory of truth kindled by
the imagination. Lamb's wide reading and memory give

G 2

a peculiar flavour to much of his wit. He had a way
of applying quotations which is all his own. When Crabb
Robinson, then a new-fledged barrister, told him of his
sensations on getting his first brief in the King's Bench,
" I suppose," said Charles, " you said to it, ' Thou great
First Cause, least understood.' "   Somebody remarking on
Shakespeare's anachronisms—clocks and watches in *Julius
Cæsar*, oracles of Delphi in the *Winter's Tale*—he said he
supposed that was what Dr. Johnson meant when he
wrote of him that " panting Time toiled after him in vain."
Hood records a visit paid by him to the Lambs when
they were living at Islington, with a wasp's nest near their
front door. " He was one day bantering my wife on her
dread of wasps, when all at once he uttered a terrible
shout—a wounded specimen of the species had slily
crawled up the leg of the table, and stung him in the
thumb. I told him it was a refutation well put in, like
Smollett's timely snowball. ' Yes,' said he, ' and a sting-
ing commentary on Macbeth,—

> By the pricking of my thumbs,
> Something wicked this way comes."

Readers of the *Essays of Elia* will recall many happy
effects produced by this novel use of familiar quotations.
Not that he ever condescended to degrade a really fine
passage by any vulgar associations. No great harm was
done (in the " Essay on Roast Pig ") by calling in his
friend's " Epitaph on an infant " to justify the sacrifice of
the innocent suckling, before it should " grow up to the
grossness and indocility which too often accompany maturer
swinehood,—

> Ere sin could blight or sorrow fade
> Death came with timely care."

And, now and then, with the true instinct of a poet, he
throws a new and lasting halo over a homely object by
associating it with one more poetic and dignified, as when
in the "Praise of Chimney-sweepers" he notes the
brilliant white of the little climbing-boys' teeth peering
from between their sooty lips—" It is," he adds—

> " as when a sable cloud
> Turns forth her silver lining on the night,"

an application of Milton which is only *not* witty, (to
borrow Sydney Smith's skilful distinction) because the
enjoyment of its wit is overpowered by our admiration of
its beauty.

"Specimens of wit and humour" afford, under the
happiest conditions, but melancholy reading, and none
can less well afford to be separated from their context than
those of Lamb.   And in his case the context is not merely
that of the written or spoken matter, but that of the man
himself—his look, manner, and habits.   To understand
how his drollery affected those who were present, and
made them anxious to preserve some record of it, it is
necessary to keep in mind how he looked and spoke, his
odd face, his stammer, and his wilfulness in the presence
of uncongenial natures.   There is a diverting scene
recorded in the diary of Haydon, the painter, which, however amplified by Haydon's facile pen, seems to bring
before us "an evening with Charles Lamb" with more
reality than the general recollections of Talfourd and
Procter.   Something of the "diluted insanity" that so
shocked Mr. Carlyle is here shadowed forth.   Haydon
had got up a little dinner, on occasion of Wordsworth
being in town (December, 1817), and Lamb and Keats
were of the party.   The account must be given in his own
words :—

On December 28th the immortal dinner came off in my painting-room, with Jerusalem towering up behind us as a background. Wordsworth was in fine cue, and we had a glorious set-to—on Homer, Shakespeare, Milton, and Virgil. Lamb got exceedingly merry, and exquisitely witty; and his fun, in the midst of Wordsworth's solemn intonations of oratory, was like the sarcasm and wit of the fool in the intervals of Lear's passion. He made a speech and voted me absent, and made them drink my health. "Now," said Lamb, "you old lake poet, you rascally poet, why do you call Voltaire dull?" We all defended Wordsworth, and affirmed there was a state of mind when Voltaire would be dull. "Well," said Lamb, "here's Voltaire—the Messiah of the French nation—and a very proper one too."

He then in a strain of humour beyond description abused me for putting Newton's head into my picture—"a fellow," said he, "who believed nothing unless it was as clear as the three sides of a triangle." And then he and Keats agreed that he had destroyed all the poetry of the rainbow, by reducing it to the prismatic colours. It was impossible to resist him, and we all drank "Newton's health, and confusion to mathematics." It was delightful to see the good humour of Wordsworth in giving in to all our frolics without affectation, and laughing as heartily as the best of us.

By this time other friends joined, amongst them poor Ritchie, who was going to penetrate by Fezzan to Timbuctoo. I introduced him to all as "a gentleman going to Africa." Lamb seemed to take no notice; but all of a sudden he roared out "Which is the gentleman we are going to lose?" We then drank the victim's health, in which Ritchie joined.

In the morning of this delightful day, a gentleman, a perfect stranger, had called on me. He said he knew my friends, had an enthusiasm for Wordsworth, and begged I would procure him the happiness of an introduction. He told me he was a Comptroller of Stamps, and often had correspondence with the poet. I thought it a liberty; but still, as he seemed a gentleman, I told him he might come.

When we retired to tea we found the Comptroller. In intro-

ducing him to Wordsworth I forgot to say who he was. After
a little time the Comptroller looked down, looked up, and said to
Wordsworth, "Don't you think, sir, Milton was a great genius?"
Keats looked at me, Wordsworth looked at the Comptroller.
Lamb, who was dozing by the fire, turned round and said,
" Pray, sir, did you say Milton was a great genius?" "No, sir,
I asked Mr. Wordsworth if he were not." "Oh," said Lamb,
"then you are a silly fellow." "Charles! my dear Charles!"
said Wordsworth; but Lamb, perfectly innocent of the con-
fusion he had created, was off again by the fire.

After an awful pause the Comptroller said, " Don't you think
Newton a great genius?" I could not stand it any longer.
Keats put his head into my books. Ritchie squeezed in a laugh.
Wordsworth seemed asking himself, " Who is this?" Lamb
got up and taking a candle, said, " Sir, will you allow me to
look at your phrenological development?" He then turned his
back on the poor man, and at every question of the Comptroller
he chanted—

> " Diddle, diddle, dumpling, my son John
> Went to bed with his breeches on."

The man in office finding Wordsworth did not know who he
was, said in a spasmodic and half-chucking anticipation of
assured victory, " I have had the honour of some correspondence
with you, Mr Wordsworth." "With me, sir?" said Wordsworth,
" not that I remember." " Don't you, sir? I am a Comptroller
of Stamps." There was a dead silence; the Comptroller evidently
thinking that was enough. While we were waiting for Wordsworth's reply, Lamb sung out—

> " Hey diddle diddle,
> The cat and the fiddle."

" My dear Charles!" said Wordsworth.

> " Diddle, diddle, dumpling, my son John,"

chanted Lamb; and then rising, exclaimed, " Do let me have

another look at that gentleman's organs." Keats and I hurried
Lamb into the painting-room, shut the door, and gave way to
inextinguishable laughter. Monkhouse followed and tried to
get Lamb away. We went back, but the Comptroller was irre-
concilable. We soothed and smiled, and asked him to supper.
He stayed, though his dignity was sorely affected. However,
being a good-natured man, we parted all in good humour, and
no ill effects followed.

All the while, until Monkhouse succeeded, we could hear
Lamb struggling in the painting-room and calling at intervals,
" Who is that fellow? Allow me to see his organs once more."

It is not difficult to guess how Carlyle or Macready
would have commented on this scene, had they been
present.

But the Wednesday evenings when Charles and Mary
Lamb kept open house—if the term could be applied to
the slender resources of the garret in Inner Temple Lane—
produced something better in the way of intellectual result
than the above. Talfourd and Procter have told us the
names and qualities of the guests who gathered about the
Lambs on these occasions, and the homely fare and the
cordial greeting that awaited them—the low, dingy rooms,
with books and prints for their chief furniture, the two
tables set out for whist, and the cold beef and can of
porter on the sideboard, to which each guest helped himself as he chose. On these occasions would be found
Wordsworth and Coleridge when in town, and then the
company resolved themselves willingly into a band of
contented listeners ; but at other times no difference of
rank would be recognized, and poets and critics, painters,
journalists, barristers, men in public offices, dramatists, and
actors met on terms of unchallenged equality. Hazlitt
has made an attempt, in a well-known essay, to reproduce

an actual conversation at which he was present on one of
these Wednesdays. He admits that, writing twenty years
after the event, memory was ill able to recall the actual
words of the speakers. But even when allowance is made
for the lapse of time, it is hard to believe that Hazlitt had
much of the Boswellian faculty. The subject that had
been discussed was "Persons one would wish to have
seen." Isaac Newton and Locke, Shakespeare and
Milton, and many others were suggested, and all dis-
missed for one reason or another by Lamb. Sir Thomas
Browne and Fulke Greville were two he substituted for
these. But it is impossible to accept the following sentence
as a sample of Lamb's conversational manner. "When
I look at that obscure but gorgeous prose composition, the
Urn Burial, I seem to myself to look into a deep abyss,
at the bottom of which are hid pearls and rich treasure;
or, it is like a stately labyrinth of doubt and withering
speculation, and I would invoke the spirit of the author
to lead me through it." This style is equally unlike that
of essay and letter, and nothing so pointless and so gran-
diose, we are sure, ever proceeded from his lips. It was
not so that Lamb, as Haydon expressed it, "stuttered out
his quaintness in snatches, like the Fool in *Lear.*" But
we can distinguish that stammering tongue, if we listen,
above the din of the supper party and the whist-table—(*not*
rigorous as Mrs. Battle's)—ranging from the maddest
drollery to the subtlest criticism, calling out to Martin
Burney, "Martin, if dirt were trumps, what a hand you'd
have,"—or declaring that he had once known a young man
who "wanted to be a tailor, but hadn't the spirit,"—or
pronouncing, *à propos* of the water-cure, that it was
neither new nor wonderful, for that it was at least as old
as the Flood, when, "in *his* opinion," it killed more than

it cured. We can hear him drawing some sound distinction, as between the ingrained jealousy of Leontes and
the mere credulity of Othello, or contrasting the noble
simplicity of the *Nut-Brown Maid* with Prior's vapid para-
phrase, in *Henry and Emma.* We can listen to him as
he fearlessly decried all his friends' idols of the hour,
Byron or Shelley or Goethe, and raved with something of
a perverse enthusiasm over some forgotten worthy of the
sixteenth century. We can hear him pleading for the
"divine compliments" of Pope, and repeating with a falter-
ing voice, the well-known lines—

> Happy my studies, when by these approved!
> Happier their author, when by these beloved!
> From these the world will judge of men and books
> Not from the Burnets, Oldmixons, and Cookes.

It was this range of sympathy, yet coupled with such
strange limitations—this alternation of tenderness and
frolic—of scholarly fulness and luminous insight, that
drew the poet and the critic, as well as the boon companion, to Lamb's Wednesday nights.

Lamb's letters at this time afford excellent specimens of
his drollery and high animal spirits. The following was
addressed to Manning early in 1810. Manning was then
in China.

DEAR MANNING.—When I last wrote you I was in lodgings.
I am now in chambers, No. 4, Inner Temple Lane, where I
should be happy to see you any evening. Bring any of your
friends, the mandarins, with you. I have two sitting-rooms; I
call them so *par excellence*, for you may stand, or loll, or lean,
or try any posture in them, but they are best for sitting; not
squatting down Japanese fashion, but the more decorous mode
which European usage has consecrated. I have two of these

rooms on the third floor, and five sleeping, cooking, &c., rooms
on the fourth floor. In my best room is a choice collection of
the works of Hogarth, an English painter of some humour. In
my next best are shelves, containing a small but well-chosen
library. My best room commands a court in which there are
trees and a pump, the water of which is excellent cold, with
brandy, and not very insipid without. Here I hope to set up my
rest, and not quit till Mr. Powell, the undertaker, gives me notice
that I may have possession of my last lodging. He lets lodgings
for single gentlemen. I sent you a parcel of books by my last, to
give you some idea of the state of European literature. There comes
with this two volumes, done up as letters, of minor poetry, a sequel
to *Mrs. Leicester ;* the best you may suppose mine; the next
best are my coadjutor's; you may amuse yourself in guessing
them out; but I must tell you mine are but one-third in quantity
of the whole. So much for a very delicate subject. It is hard
to speak of one's own self, &c. Holcroft had finished his life
when I wrote to you, and Hazlitt has since finished his life: I
do not mean his own life, but he has finished a life of Holcroft,
which is going to press. Tuthill is Dr. Tuthill; I continue
Mr. Lamb. I have published a little book for children on titles
of honour; and to give them some idea of the difference of
rank and gradual rising I have made a little scale, supposing
myself to receive the following various accessions of dignity from
the king, who is the fountain of honour. As at first, 1, Mr. C.
Lamb; 2, C. Lamb, Esq.; 3, Sir C. Lamb, Bart.; 4, Baron
Lamb of Stamford [1]; 5, Viscount Lamb; 6, Earl Lamb; 7,
Marquis Lamb; 8, Duke Lamb. It would look like quibbling
to carry it on further, and especially as it is not necessary for
children to go beyond the ordinary titles of sub-regal dignity in
our own country; otherwise, I have sometimes in my dreams
imagined myself still advancing—as 9th, King Lamb; 10th,
Emperor Lamb; 11th, Pope Innocent, higher than which is
nothing. Puns I have not made many (nor punch much) since

[1] Where my family came from. I have chosen that, if ever I
should have my choice.

the date of my last; one I cannot help relating. A constable
in Salisbury Cathedral was telling me that eight people dined at
the top of the spire of the cathedral, upon which I remarked
that they must be very sharp set. But in general, I cultivate
the reasoning part of my mind more than the imaginative. I
am stuffed out so with eating turkey for dinner and another
turkey for supper yesterday (Turkey in Europe and Turkey in
Asia), that I can't jog on. It is New Year here. That is, it
was New Year half a year back when I was writing this.
Nothing puzzles me more than time and space, and yet nothing
puzzles me less, for I never think about them. The Persian
ambassador is the principal thing talked of now. I sent some
people to see him worship the sun on Primrose Hill, at half-
past six in the morning, 28th November; but he did not come,
which makes me think the old fire-worshippers are a sect almost
extinct in Persia. The Persian ambassador's name is Shaw
Ali Mirza. The common people call him Shaw nonsense.
While I think of it, I have put three letters besides my own
three into the India post for you, from your brother, sister, and
some gentleman whose name I forget. Will they, have they,
did they come safe? The distance you are at cuts up tenses by the
root. I think you said you did not know Kate * * * * * * * * *.
I express her by nine stars, though she is but one. You must
have seen her at her father's. Try and remember her. Coleridge is bringing out a paper in weekly numbers, called the
Friend, which I would send if I could; but the difficulty I had
in getting the packets of books out to you before deters me;
and you'll want something new to read when you come home.
Except Kate, I have had no vision of excellence this year, and
she passed by like the queen on her coronation day; you don't
know whether you saw her or not. Kate is fifteen; I go about
moping, and sing the old pathetic ballad I used to like in my
youth—

> She's sweet fifteen,
> I'm *one year more.*

Mrs. Bland sang it in boy's clothes the first time I heard it. I

sometimes think the lower notes in my voice are like Mrs.
Bland's. That glorious singer, Braham, one of my lights, is
fled. He was for a season. He was a rare composition of the
Jew, the gentleman, and the angel; yet all these elements mixed
up so kindly in him that you could not tell which preponderated;
but he is gone, and one Phillips is engaged instead. Kate is
vanished, but Miss B—— is always to be met with!

> Queens drop away, while blue-legged maukin thrives,
> And courtly Mildred dies while country Madge survives.

That is not my poetry, but Quarles'; but haven't you observed
that the rarest things are the least obvious? Don't show any-
body the names in this letter. I write confidentially, and wish
this letter to be considered as *private*. Hazlitt has written a
grammar for Godwin; Godwin sells it bound up with a treatise
of his own on language, but the *grey mare is the better horse.*
I don't allude to Mrs. —— but to the word grammar, which
comes near to *grey mare*, if you observe, in sound. That figure
is called paranomasia in Greek. I am sometimes happy in it.
An old woman begged of me for charity. " Ah! sir," said she,
"I have seen better days." "So have I, good woman," I replied;
but I meant literally, days not so rainy and overcast as that on
which she begged; she meant more prosperous days. Mr. Dawe
is made Associate of the Royal Academy. By what law of
association I can't guess.

The humour of this letter—and there are many as good
—is not the humour of the *Essays of Elia*. It is not
charged with thought like them, nor does it reach the
same depths of feeling. But it is the humour of a man
of genius. The inventiveness of it all; the simplicity
with which the most daring flights of fancy are hazarded;
the amazing improbability of the assertion that it was the
" common people " who called the ambassador " Shaw
nonsense ;" the gravity with which it is set down that it is
not necessary *in England* to teach children the degrees

of rank beyond royalty,—all this is delightful in the extreme, and the power to enjoy it may be taken as a test of the reader's capacity for understanding Lamb's place as a humorist.

The eight years spent in Inner Temple Lane were, in Talfourd's judgment, the happiest of Lamb's life. His income was steadily rising, and he no longer had to bear the pressure of inconvenient poverty. Friends of a higher order than the " friendly harpies " he has told us of, who came about him for his suppers, and the brandy-and-water afterwards, were gradually gathering round him. Hazlitt, and Crabb Robinson, and Procter, and Talfourd were men of tastes and capacities akin to his own. The period was not a fertile one in literary production. The little collection of stories for children, called *Mrs. Leicester's School,* written jointly with his sister, and the volume of *Poetry for Children*, also a joint production, constitute—with one notable exception—the whole of Lamb's literary labours during this time. The exception named is the contribution to Leigh Hunt's periodical, the *Reflector*, of two or three masterly pieces of criticism, which may be more conveniently noticed later in this memoir.

Meantime the cloud of domestic anxiety was still unlifted. Mary Lamb's illnesses were frequent and embarrassing. An extract from a letter to Miss Hutchinson, Mrs. Wordsworth's sister (October, 1815), tells once more the often-told tale, and shows the unaltered patience and seriousness of her brother's faithful guardianship. The passage has a further interest in the picture it incidentally draws of the happier days of the brother and sister :—

" I am forced to be the replier to your letter, for Mary has been ill, and gone from home these five weeks yesterday. She has left me very lonely and very miserable. I stroll

about, but there is no rest but at one's own fireside, and
there is no rest for me there now. I look forward to the
worse half being past, and keep up as well as I can. She
has begun to show some favourable symptoms. The
return of her disorder has been frightfully soon this time,
with scarce a six months' interval. I am almost afraid
my worry of spirits about the East India House was partly
the cause of her illness, but one always imputes it to the
cause next at hand ; more probably it comes from some
cause we have no control over or conjecture of. It cuts
great slices out of the time, the little time, we shall have to
live together. I don't know but the recurrence of these
illnesses might help me to sustain her death better than if
we had no partial separations. But I won't talk of death.
I will imagine us immortal, or forget that we are otherwise. By God's blessing, in a few weeks we may be
making our meal together, or sitting in the front row of
the Pit at Drury Lane, or taking our evening walk past the
theatres, to look at the outside of them, at least, if not to
be tempted in. Then we forget that we are assailable ; we
are strong for the time as rocks ;—' the wind is tempered to
the shorn Lambs. ' "

CHAPTER VI.

(1817—1823.)

In the autumn of 1817, Lamb and his sister left the Temple, their home for seventeen years, for lodgings in Great Russell Street, Covent Garden, the corner of Bow Street, and the site where Will's Coffee-House once stood. " Here we are," Lamb writes to Miss Wordsworth in November of this year, " transplanted from our native soil. I thought we never could have been torn up from the Temple. Indeed it was an ugly wrench, but like a tooth, now 'tis out, and I am easy. We never can strike root so deep in any other ground. This, where we are, is a light bit of gardener's mould, and if they take us up from it, it will cost no blood and groans, like mandrakes pulled up. We are in the individual spot I like best in all this great city. The theatres with all their noises; Covent Garden, dearer to me than any gardens of Alcinous, where we are morally sure of the earliest peas and 'sparagus. Bow Street, where the thieves are examined within a few yards of us. Mary had not been here four-and-twenty hours before she saw a thief. She sits at the window working; and casually throwing out her eyes, she sees a concourse of people coming this way, with a constable to conduct the solemnity. These little incidents agreeably diversify a female life."

During the seventeen years in the Temple, Lamb's worldly fortunes had improved. His salary from the India House was increasing every year, and he was beginning to add to his income by authorship. He was already known as critic and essayist to an appreciative few. Friends were gathering round him, and acquaintances who enjoyed his conversation and his weekly suppers (Wednesday evening was open house in the Temple days) were increasing in rather an embarrassing degree. Ever since he had had a house of his own, he had suffered from the intrusion of such troublesome visitors. A too easy good-nature on his part may have been to blame for this. He took often, as he confesses, a perverse pleasure in noticing and befriending those whom others, with good reason, looked shyly on, and as time went on he began to find very little of his leisure time that he could call his own. It may have been with some hope of beginning a freer life on new soil that he resolved to tear himself from his beloved Temple. If so he was not successful. A remarkable letter to Mrs. Wordsworth, a few months only after his removal to Russell Street, tells the same old story of well-meaning intruders. "The reason why I cannot write letters at home is that I am never alone." "Except my morning's walk to the office, which is like treading on sands of gold for that reason, I am never so. I cannot walk home from office, but some officious friend offers his unwelcome courtesies to accompany me. All the morning I am pestered. Evening company I should always like, had I any mornings, but I am saturated with human faces (*divine* forsooth), and voices all the golden morning; and five evenings in a week would be as much as I should

H

covet to be in company, but I assure you that it is a wonderful week in which I can get two, or one to myself. I
am never C. L. but always C. L. & Co. He, who thought
it not good for man to be alone, preserve me from the
more prodigious monstrosity of being never by myself."
" All I mean is that I am a little over-companied, but
not that I have any animosity against the good creatures
that are so anxious to drive away the harpy solitude from
me. I like 'em, and cards, and a cheerful glass ; but I
mean merely to give you an idea between office confinement
and after-office society, how little time I can call my own."
It is not difficult to form an idea from this frank dis-
closure, of the hindrances and the snares that beset Lamb's
comfort and acted harmfully on his temper and habits.
It was fortunate for him that at this juncture he should
have been led to discover where his powers as a writer
indisputably lay, and to find the exact opportunity for their
exercise.

In this same year, 1818, a young bookseller, Charles
Ollier, whose acquaintance he had recently made, proposed
to him to bring out a complete collection of his scattered
writings. Some of these, *John Woodvil* and *Rosamond
Gray*, had been published separately in former years, and
were now out of print. Others were interred among extinct
magazines and journals, and these were by far the most
worthy of preservation. The edition appeared in the year
1818, in two handsome volumes. It contained, besides
John Woodvil and *Rosamond Gray*, and a fair quantity of
verse (including the *Farewell to Tobacco*), the *Recollections of Christ's Hospital*, the essay on *The Tragedies of
Shakespeare, considered with reference to their fitness for
stage representation*, and that on *The Genius and Character
of Hogarth*, these two last having originally appeared in

Leigh Hunt's magazine, the *Reflector*. The edition was pre-
faced by a dedicatory letter to Coleridge. "You will smile,"
wrote Lamb, "to see the slender labours of your friend
designated by the title of *Works ;* but such was the wish
of the gentlemen who have kindly undertaken the trouble
of collecting them, and from their judgment there could
be no appeal." He goes on pleasantly to recall to his old
schoolfellow how, in company with their friend Lloyd,
they had so many years before tried their poetical fortune.
"You will find your old associate," he adds, "in his second
volume, dwindled into prose and *criticism.*" Lamb
must have felt, as he wrote the word, that "dwindled"
was hardly the fitting term. He had written nothing
as yet so noble in matter and in style, nothing so worthy
to live, as the analysis of the characters of Hamlet and Lear
in the essay on *Shakespeare's Tragedies.* Lamb's high rank,
as essayist and critic, must have been put beyond dispute
by the publication under his own name of his collected
Works. He was already well known and appreciated by
some of the finest minds of his day. He now addressed a
wider public, and the edition of 1818 gave him a status he
had not before enjoyed. And yet at this date, various as
were the contents of the two volumes, he had not found
the opportunity that was to call forth his special faculty.

The opportunity was, however, at hand. In January
1820, Baldwin, Cradock, and Joy, the publishers, brought
out the first number of a new monthly journal, reviving in
it the name of an earlier, and extinct periodical, the *London
Magazine.* The editor they chose was John Scott, a com-
petent critic and journalist who had formerly edited the
Champion newspaper. The aim of this new venture, as
set forth in the opening prospectus, was to be of a higher
and more intellectual class than its many popular contem-

poraries. It was to be a journal of criticism and the
Belles Lettres, including original poetry, and yet to contain
in a monthly appendix such statistics of trade and general
home and foreign intelligence as would make it useful to
those of a less literary turn. The magazine had an existence
of five years, undergoing many changes of fortune, and
passing in that time through many hands. Its first
editor, Mr. Scott, was killed in a duel in the summer of
1821, and its first publishers parted with it to Taylor and
Hessey. At no period of its career does it seem to have
been a marked commercial success. Either capital was
wanted, or management was unsatisfactory, for the list of
contributors during these five years was remarkable. Mr.
Procter and Hood have discoursed pleasantly on their
various fellow-contributors to the magazine, and the social
gatherings held once a month by Taylor and Hessey (who
employed no editor) at the office in Waterloo Place.
Hazlitt, Allan Cunningham, Cary (the translator of
Dante), John Hamilton Reynolds, George Darley,
Keats, James Montgomery, Sir John Bowring, Hartley
Coleridge, were regular or occasional contributors. Carlyle
published his *Life and Writings of Schiller* in the later
volumes, and De Quincey (besides other papers) his *Opium
Eater*.

Talfourd thinks that Lamb owed to his intimacy with
Hazlitt his introduction to the managers of the *London*.
He was not on the staff from the beginning. The
first number was issued in January 1820, and Lamb's
first contribution was in the August following. In the
number for that month appeared an article, with the not
very attractive title, *Recollections of the South-Sea House*.
As to its authorship there was no indication except the
signature at the end—" Elia." Lamb has himself told us

the origin of this immortal *nom de plume.* When he had
written his first essay, wishing to remain anonymous, and
yet wanting a convenient mark for identification in articles
to come, he bethought him of an Italian of the name of
Elia, who had been fellow-clerk with him thirty years
before, during the few months that he had been employed
as a boy in the South-Sea House. As a practical joke
(Lamb confesses) he borrowed his old friend's name,
hoping to make his excuses when they should next meet.
"I went the other day," writes Lamb in June 1821,
" (not having seen him for a year) to laugh over with him
at my usurpation of his name, and found him, alas! no
more than a name, for he died of consumption eleven
months ago, and I knew not of it. So the name has
fairly devolved to me, I think, and 'tis all he has left me."
Lamb continued to use it for his contributions to the
London and other periodicals for many years.   It is doubt-
ful if the name has ever been generally pronounced as
Lamb intended.   "Call him Ellia," he wrote to his publisher, Mr. Taylor, but the world has taken more kindly to
the broad e and the single l.

When the first series of the *Essays of Elia* appeared in
a collected form in 1823, it consisted of some five-and-
twenty essays, contributed at the rate of one a month
(occasionally two) with scarcely an intermission between
August, 1820, and December, 1822.   It would seem as if
no conditions had been imposed upon Lamb by the editor
as to the subject-matter of his essays.   He was allowed to
roam at his own free will over the experiences of his life,
and to reproduce them in any form, and with any discur-
siveness into which he might be allured on the way.   The
matter of the essays proved to be largely personal, or at
least to savour of the autobiographical.   The first essay

already referred to professed to be a recollection of the
South-Sea House as it existed thirty years before, with
sketches of several of the clerks who had been
Lamb's contemporaries. As, however, he was a boy of
fifteen at the time he entered, and moreover was at most
two years in the office, it is probable that he owed much of
the knowledge exhibited in the paper to his elder brother
John, who remained in the office long after Charles had left
it. Lamb was in the habit of spending his short summer
holiday in one or other of the two great University towns,
and his second essay was an account of *Oxford in the Vacation.* The third in order of appearance was an account of
Christ's Hospital, on that side of it which had *not* been
touched in his earlier paper on the same subject. The
fourth was a discursive meditation on the *Two Races of
Men,* by which Lamb meant those who borrow and those
who lend, which he illustrated by the example of one
Ralph Bigod (whom he had known in his journalist days
on the *Albion*), and Coleridge, who so freely borrowed
from Lamb's library, and so bountifully returned the
loan with interest in the shape of marginal annotations.
In the essay, *Mrs. Battle's Opinions on Whist,* he
describes an old lady, a relative of the Plumer family,
whom he had known in person, or by repute, at the old
mansion in Hertfordshire. In the chapter *On Ears,* his
own want of musical ear, and the kind of impressions
from musical sounds to which he was susceptible, is the
subject of his confidences. In *My Relations,* and *Mackery
End in Hertfordshire* he draws portraits, under the disguise of two cousins, James and Bridget Elia, of his
brother John and his sister Mary. *The Old Benchers of
the Inner Temple* comprises all that he remembered of his
boyhood spent in the Temple, with particulars of the

more notable Masters of the Bench of that day, obtained
no doubt from his father, the Lovel of the essay, and his
father's old and loyal friend Randal Norris, the sub-
treasurer of the Inner Temple.   Other essays, such as that
On Chimney Sweepers, and *The Decay of Beggars in the
Metropolis*, contain the results of that observing eye with
which he had daily surveyed the streets of his beloved
city for so many years, " looking no one in the face for
more than a moment," as Mr. Procter has told us, yet
" contriving to see everything as he went on."

The opening essay on the *South-Sea House* shows that
there was no need to feel his way, either in matter or
style.   He began in the fulness of his observation, and
with a style already formed, and adapting itself to all
changes of thought and feeling.   His description of John
Tipp, the accountant, was enough to show that not only a
keen observer, but a master of English was at work :—

At the desk, Tipp was quite another sort of creature.   Thence
all ideas that were purely ornamental were banished.   You
could not speak of anything romantic without rebuke.   Politics
were excluded.   A newspaper was thought too refined and
abstracted.   The whole duty of man consisted in writing off
dividend warrants.   The striking of the annual balance in the
company's books (which perhaps differed from the balance of
last year in the sum of 25*l.* 1*s.* 6*d.*) occupied his days and nights
for a month previous.   Not that Tipp was blind to the deadness
of *things* (as they call them in the city) in his beloved house, or
did not sigh for a return of the old stirring days when South-
Sea hopes were young (he was indeed equal to the wielding of
any the most intricate accounts of the most flourishing company
in these or those days) : but to a genuine accountant the difference of proceeds is as nothing.   The fractional farthing is as dear
to his heart as the thousands which stand before it.   He is the
true actor who, whether his part be a prince or a peasant, must

act it with like intensity. With Tipp, form was everything. His life was formal. His actions seemed ruled with a ruler. His pen was not less erring than his heart. He made the best executor in the world; he was plagued with incessant executor- ships accordingly, which excited his spleen and soothed his vanity in equal ratios. He would swear (for Tipp swore) at the little orphans, whose rights he would guard with a tenacity like the grasp of the dying hand that commended their interests to his protection. With all this there was about him a sort of timidity—his few enemies used to give it a worse name—a something which, in reverence to the dead, we will place, if you please, a little on this side of the heroic. Nature certainly had been pleased to endow John Tipp with a sufficient measure of the principle of self-preservation. There is a cowardice which we do not despise, because it has nothing base or treacherous in its elements; it betrays itself, not you; it is mere temperament; the absence of the romantic and the enterprising; it sees a lion in the way, and will not, with Fortinbras, "greatly find quarrel in a straw," when some supposed honour is at stake. Tipp never mounted the box of a stage coach in his life, or leaned against the rails of a balcony, or walked upon the ridge of a parapet, or looked down a precipice, or let off a gun, or went upon a water- party, or would willingly let you go if he could have helped it; neither was it recorded of him that for lucre, or for intimidation, he ever forsook friend or principle.

Two of the essays have attained a celebrity, certainly not out of proportion to their merits, but serving to make quotation from them almost an impertinence. These are the *Dissertation on Roast Pig*, Lamb's version of a story told him by his friend Manning (though *not* probably to be found in any Chinese manuscript), and the essay, finally called *Imperfect Sympathies*, but originally bearing the cumbrous title of *Jews, Quakers, Scotchmen, and other Imperfect Sympathies*. It is here that occurs the famous analysis of the Scotch character, perhaps the cleverest

passage, in its union of fine observation and felicity of
phrase, in the whole of Lamb's writings.   The anecdote of
Lamb's favourite picture,—his "beauty,"—the Lionardo da
Vinci, and that of the party where the son of Burns was
expected, together with the complaint that follows of the
hopelessness of satisfying a Scotchman in the matter of
the appreciation of that poet, have become as much
commonplaces of quotation as Sydney Smith's famous
reference to the surgical operation.   The brilliancy of the
whole passage has rather thrown into the shade the dis-
quisition on Quaker manners that follows, and the story
he had heard from Carlisle, the surgeon, of the three
Quakers who "stopped to bait" at Andover.   But the
whole paper is excellent.

Hardly less familiar is the account of old Mrs. Battle,
and her opinions upon the game of whist.   "'A clear fire,
a clean hearth, and the rigour of the game.'   This was the
celebrated wish of old Sarah Battle (now with God) who next
to her devotions loved a good game at whist.   She was none
of your lukewarm gamesters, your half and half players, who
have no objection to take a hand if you want one to make
up a rubber ; who affirm that they have no pleasure in
winning, that they like to win one game and lose another,
that they can while away an hour very agreeably at a card-
table, but are indifferent whether they play or no, and will
desire an adversary who has slipped a wrong card to take
it up and play another.   These insufferable triflers are the
curse of a table ; one of these flies will spoil a whole pot.
Of such it may be said that they do not play at cards, but
only play at playing with them."

The portrait must have been drawn in the main from
life.   One of the most singular suggestions ever offered by
Lamb's editors is that this "gentlewoman born," with her

"fine last-century countenance," the niece of "old Walter
Plumer," was drawn from Lamb's old grandmother, Mrs.
Field.   As a test of the likelihood of this theory it will be
found instructive to read, after this essay, the touching
lines already cited called *The Grandame*.

The marked peculiarities of Lamb's style give so unique
a colouring to all these essays that one is apt to overlook to what a variety of themes it is found suitable.
There is no mood, from that of almost reckless merriment to that of pathetic sweetness or religious awe,
to which the style is not able to modulate with no felt
sense of incongruity.   A feature of Lamb's method, as
we have seen, is his use of quotations.   Not only are
they brought in so as really to illustrate, but the passages
cited themselves receive illustration from the use made of
them, and gain a permanent and heightened value from it.
Whether it be a garden-scene from Marvell, a solemn paradox from Sir Thomas Browne, or a stanza from some then
recent poem of Wordsworth, the quotation fulfils a double
purpose, and has sent many a reader to explore for himself
in the author whose words strike him with such luminous
effect in their new setting.   Take, for example, the
Miltonic digression in the essay on *Grace before Meat*.
Lamb is never more happy than in quoting from or dis-
coursing on Milton:—

The severest satire upon full tables and surfeits is the banquet which Satan, in the *Paradise Regained*, provides for a
temptation in the wilderness :—

> A table richly spread in regal modes
> With dishes piled and meats of noblest sort
> And savour ; beasts of chase, or fowl of game,
> In pastry built, or from the spit, or boiled
> Gris-amber-steamed ; all fish from sea or shore,
> Freshet or purling brook, for which was drained
> Pontus, and Lucrine bay, and Afric coast.

The tempter, I warrant you, thought these cates would go down without the recommendatory preface of a benediction. They are like to be short graces where the devil plays the host. I am afraid the poet wants his usual decorum in this place. Was he thinking of the old Roman luxury, or of a gaudy day at Cambridge? This was a temptation fitter for a Heliogabalus. The whole banquet is too civic and culinary; and the accompaniments altogether a profanation of that deep, abstracted, holy scene. The mighty artillery of sauces which the cook-fiend conjures up, is out of proportion to the simple wants and plain hunger of the guest. He that disturbed him in his dreams, from his dreams might have been taught better. To the temperate fantasies of the famished Son of God what sort of feasts presented themselves? He dreamed indeed—

> As appetite is wont to dream
> Of meats and drinks, nature's refreshment sweet.

But what meats?

> Him thought, he by the brook of Cherith stood,
> And saw the ravens with their horny beaks
> Food to Elijah bringing even and morn:
> Though ravenous, taught to abstain from what they brought.
> He saw the prophet also how he fled
> Into the desert, and how there he slept
> Under a juniper: then how awaked
> He found his supper on the coals prepared,
> And by the angel was bid rise and eat,
> And ate the second time after repose,
> The strength whereof sufficed him forty days:
> Sometimes, that with Elijah he partook
> Or as a guest with Daniel at his pulse.

Nothing in Milton is finelier fancied than these temperate dreams of the divine Hungerer. To which of these two visionary banquets, think you, would the introduction of what is called the grace have been most fitting and pertinent?

"I am no Quaker at my food." So Lamb characteristically proceeds, after one short paragraph interposed.

"I confess I am not indifferent to the kinds of it. Those unctuous morsels of deer's flesh were not made to be received with dispassionate services. I hate a man who swallows it, affecting not to know what he is eating; I suspect his taste in higher matters. I shrink instinctively from one who professes to like minced veal. There is a physiognomical character in the tastes for food. C—— holds that a man cannot have a pure mind who refuses apple-dumplings. I am not certain but he is right."

And so he rambles on in almost endless digression and absolute fearlessness as to egotism of such a kind ever palling or annoying. This egotism—it is almost super-fluous to mark—is a dominant characteristic of Lamb's manner. The prominence of the personal element had indeed been a feature of the essay proper ever since Montaigne, its first inventor. But Lamb's use of the "I" has little resemblance to the gossiping confessions of the Gascon gentleman. These grave avowals as to the minced veal and the dumplings are not of the same order as Montaigne's confidences as to his preference of white wine to red. The "I" of Lamb in such a case is no concession to an idle curiosity, nor is it in fact biographical at all. Nor is it the egotism of Steele and Addison, though, when occasion arises, Lamb shows signs of the influence upon him of these earlier masters in his own special school. He thus begins, for instance, his paper called *The Wedding :*— "I do not know when I have been better pleased than at being invited last week to be present at the wedding of a friend's daughter. I like to make one at these ceremonies, which to us old people give back our youth in a manner, and restore our gayest season, in the remembrance of our own success, or the regrets scarcely less tender, of our own youthful disappointments, in this point of a settlement.

On these occasions I am sure to be in good-humour for a
week or two after, and enjoy a reflected honeymoon."
In matter, language, and cadence, this might have been
taken bodily from the *Spectator*. Yet this was no freak
of imitation on Lamb's part. It merely arose from the
subject and the train of thought engendered by it being of
that domestic kind which Richard Steele loved so well to
discourse on. Lamb's mind and memory were so stored
with English reading of an older date, that the occurrence
of a particular theme sends him back, quite naturally, to
those early masters who had specially made that theme
their own. For all his strongly-marked individuality of
manner, there are perhaps few English writers who have
written so differently upon different themes. When he
chose to be fanciful, he could be as euphuistic as Donne
or Burton—when he was led to be grave and didactic, he
could write with the sententiousness of Bacon,—when
his imagination and feeling together lifted him above
thoughts of style, his English cleared and soared into
regions not far below the noblest flights of Milton and
Jeremy Taylor. When on the other hand he was at home,
on homely themes, he wrote " like a man of this world,"
and of his own century and year.

Still it must be said that his style is in the main an
eclectic English. It is needless to add that this implies
no affectation. No man ever wrote to such purpose in a
style deliberately assumed. Hazlitt remarks of him, that
" he is so thoroughly imbued with the spirit of his authors,
that the idea of imitation is almost done way. There is
an inward unction, a marrowy vein both in the thought
and feeling, an intuition, deep and lively, of his subject
that carries off any quaintness or awkwardness arising
from an antiquated style and dress." This is quite true,

and Hazlitt might have added that in the rare instances when Lamb used this old fashioned manner, without the deeper thought or finer observation to elevate it, the manner alone, whimsical and ingenious as it is, becomes a trifle wearisome. The euphuistic ingenuity of *All Fools' Day* is not a pleasing sample of Lamb's faculty.

His friend Bernard Barton wrote of him in a sonnet,

> From the olden time
> Of authorship, thy patent should be dated,
> And thou with Marvell, Browne, and Burton, mated.

This trio of authors is well chosen. There is no poet he loves better to quote than Marvell, and none with whose poetic vein his own is more in sympathy. Lamb received his impressions from nature (unless it was in Hertfordshire) largely through the medium of books, and he makes it clear that old-fashioned garden-scenes come to him first with their peculiar charm when he meets with them in Milton or Marvell. But the second name cited by Barton is the most important of all among the influences on Lamb's style and the cast of his thought. Of all old writers, the author of the *Urn Burial* and the *Religio Medici* appears oftenest, in quotation or allusion, in the *Essays of Elia*. Lamb somewhere boasts that he first "among the moderns" discovered and proclaimed his excellences. And though Lamb never (so far as I can discover) caught the special rhythm of Browne's sentences, it is from him that he adopted the constant habit just referred to, of asserting his opinions, feelings, and speculations in the first person. Different as are the two men in other regards, Lamb's egotism is largely the egotism of Sir Thomas Browne. From Browne too he probably caught a certain habit of gloomy paradox, in dwelling on

the mysteries of the supernatural world. His sombre
musings upon death in the essay called *New Year's Eve*
bear the strong impress of Browne, notwithstanding that
they are antagonistic (perhaps consciously) to a remarkable passage in the *Religio Medici.* And even in his
lighter vein of speculation, Lamb's persistent use of the
first person often reads as if he were humorously parody-
ing the same original.

A large portion of Lamb's history is related in these
essays, and with the addition of a few names and dates, a
complete biography might be constructed from them alone.
As we have seen, he tells of his childish thoughts and
feelings, of his school-days, his home in the Temple, the
Hertfordshire village where he passed his holidays as a
boy, and the University towns where he loved to spend
them in manhood. He has drawn most detailed portraits of his grandmother, his father, sister, and brother,
and would no doubt have added that of his mother, but
for the painful memories it would have brought to Mary.
Of the incidents in the happier days of his life, when Mary
was in good health, and the daily sharer in all interests
and pleasures, he has written with a special charm. There
is a passage in the essay called *Old China* without which
any picture of their united life would be incomplete.
The essay had begun by declaring Lamb's partiality for
old china, from which after a few paragraphs he diverges,
by a modulation common with him, to the recollection
of his past struggles. He had been taking tea, he says,
with his cousin (under this relationship his sister Mary
is always indicated), using a new set of china, and
remarking to her on their better fortunes which enabled
them to indulge now and again in the luxury of such
a purchase, "when a passing sentiment seemed to overshade

the brows of my companion. I am quick at detecting these
summer clouds in Bridget.

" I wish the good old times would come again," she
said, " when we were not quite so rich. I do not mean
that I want to be poor, but there was a middle state," so
she was pleased to ramble on, " in which I am sure we
were a great deal happier. A purchase is but a purchase,
now that you have money enough and to spare. Formerly it used to be a triumph. When we coveted a cheap
luxury (and O ! how much ado I had to get you to con-
sent in those days !) we were used to have a debate two or
three days before, and to weigh the *for* and *against*, and
think what we might spare it out of, and what saving we
could hit upon, that should be an equivalent. A thing was
worth buying then, when we felt the money that we paid
for it.

" Do you remember the brown suit which you made to
hang upon you, till all your friends cried shame upon you,
it grew so threadbare, and all because of that folio Beaumont and Fletcher, which you dragged home late at night
from Barker's in Covent Garden ? Do you remember how
we eyed it for weeks before we could make up our minds
to the purchase, and had not come to a determination till
it was near ten o'clock of the Saturday night, when you
set off from Islington fearing you should be too late—and
when the old bookseller, with some grumbling opened his
shop, and by the twinkling taper (for he was setting bed-
wards), lighted out the relic from his dusty treasures, and
when you lugged it home, wishing it were twice as cum-
bersome, and when you presented it to me, and when we
were exploring the perfectness of it (*collating*, you called
it), and while I was repairing some of the loose leaves
with paste, which your impatience would not suffer to be

left till daybreak—was there no pleasure in being a poor
man? or can those neat black clothes which you wear now,
and are so careful to keep brushed, since we have become
rich and finical, give you half the honest vanity with
which you flaunted it about in that over-worn suit—your
old corbeau—for four or five weeks longer than you should
have done, to pacify your conscience for the mighty sum
of fifteen or sixteen shillings, was it?—a great affair we
thought it then—which you had lavished on the old
folio? Now you can afford to buy any book that pleases
you, but I do not see that you ever bring me home any
nice old purchases now."

The essay " Blakesmoor in H——shire " has been more
than once referred to, in connexion with Lamb's old
grandmother, Mrs. Field.   The essay acquires a new
interest when it is known how much of fact is contained in it. William Plumer, who represented his
county in parliament for so many years, and was at the
time of his death in 1822, member for Higham Ferrers,
left his estates at Gilston and Blakesware to his widow,
apparently with the understanding that the old Blakesware mansion should be pulled down. Accordingly not
long before the date of Lamb's essay (September, 1824) it
had been levelled to the ground; and some of the more
valuable of its contents, including the busts of the Twelve
Cæsars, so often dwelt on by Lamb in letter or essay,
removed to the other house at Gilston. Under its roof,
and among its gardens and terraces, Lamb's happiest days
as a child had been spent, and he had just been to look
once more on the few vestiges still remaining :—

I do not know a pleasure more affecting than to range at will
over the deserted apartments of some fine old family mansion.

I

The traces of extinct grandeur admit of a better passion than envy; and contemplations on the great and good, whom we fancy in succession to have been its inhabitants, weave for us illusions incompatible with the bustle of modern occupancy, and vanities of foolish present aristocracy. The same difference of feeling, I think, attends us between entering an empty and a crowded church. In the latter it is chance but some present human frailty—an act of inattention on the part of some of the auditory, or a trait of affectation, or worse, vainglory, on that of the preacher—puts us by our best thoughts, disharmonizing the place and the occasion. But would'st thou know the beauty of holiness? Go alone on some weekday, borrowing the keys of good Master Sexton, traverse the cool aisles of some country church; think of the piety that has kneeled there—the congregations, old and young, that have found consolation there—the meek pastor, the docile parishioner. With no disturbing emotions, no cross, conflicting comparisons, drink in the tranquillity of the place, till thou thyself become as fixed and motionless as the marble effigies that kneel and weep around thee.

Journeying northward lately, I could not resist going some few miles out of my road to look upon the remains of an old great house with which I had been impressed in this way in infancy. I was apprised that the owner of it had lately pulled it down; still I had a vague notion that it could not all have perished, that so much solidity with magnificence could not have been crushed all at once into the mere dust and rubbish which I found it.

The work of ruin had proceeded with a swift hand indeed, and the demolition of a few weeks had reduced it to an antiquity.

I was astonished at the indistinction of everything. Where had stood the great gates? What bounded the courtyard? Whereabout did the outhouses commence? A few bricks only lay as representatives of that which was so stately and so spacious.

Death does not shrink up his human victim at this rate. The burnt ashes of a man weigh more in their proportion.

Had I seen these brick and mortar knaves at their process of destruction, at the plucking of every panel I should have felt the varlets at my heart. I should have cried out to them to spare a plank at least out of the cheerful store-room, in whose hot window-seat I used to sit and read Cowley, with the grass-plot before, and the hum and flappings of that one solitary wasp that ever haunted it about me—it is in mine ears now, as oft as summer returns ; or a panel of the yellow room.

Why, every plank and panel of that house for me had magic in it. The tapestried bedrooms—tapestry so much better than painting—not adorning merely—but peopling the wainscots— at which childhood ever and anon would steal a look, shifting its coverlid (replaced as quickly) to exercise its tender courage in a momentary eye-encounter with those stern bright visages, staring reciprocally—all Ovid on the walls—in colours vivider than his descriptions. Actæon in mid sprout, with the unappeasable prudery of Diana; and the still more provoking and almost culinary coolness of Dan Phœbus, eel-fashion, deliberately divesting of Marsyas.

Then that haunted room—in which old Mrs. Battle died—whereinto I have crept, but always in the daytime, with a passion of fear ; and a sneaking curiosity, terror-tainted, to hold communication with the past.—*How shall they build it up again ?*

It was an old deserted place, yet not so long deserted but that traces of the splendour of past inmates were everywhere apparent. Its furniture was still standing, even to the tarnished gilt-leather battledores and crumbling feathers of shuttlecocks in the nursery, which told that children had once played there. But I was a lonely child, and had the range at will of every apartment, knew every nook and corner, wondered and worshipped everywhere. The solitude of childhood is not so much the mother of thought, as it is the feeder of love, and silence, and admiration. So strange a passion for the place possessed me in those years, that though there lay—I shame to say how few roods distant from the mansion—half hid by trees, what I judged some romantic lake, such was the spell which bound me to the house, and such my carefulness not to pass its strict and

proper precincts, that the idle waters lay unexplored for me ;
and not till late in life, curiosity prevailing over elder devotion,
I found, to my astonishment, a pretty brawling brook had been
the Lacus Incognitus of my infancy. Variegated views, ex-
tensive prospects—and those at no great distance from the house
—I was told of such—what were they to me, being out of the
boundaries of my Eden ? So far from a wish to roam, I would
have drawn, methought, still closer the fences of my chosen
prison ; and have been hemmed in by a yet securer cincture of
those excluding garden walls. I could have exclaimed with that
garden-loving poet—

> Bind me, ye woodbines, in your twines ;
> Curl me about, ye gadding vines ;
> And oh so close your circles lace,
> That I may never leave this place :
> But lest your fetters prove too weak,
> Ere I your silken bondage break,
> Do you, O brambles, chain me too,
> And, courteous briars, nail me through.[1]

I was here as in a lonely temple. Snug firesides, the low-
built roof, parlours ten feet by ten, frugal boards, and all the
homeliness of home—these were the condition of my birth—the
wholesome soil which I was planted in.

Yet without impeachment to their tenderest lessons, I am not
sorry to have had glances of something beyond ; and to have
taken, if but a peep, in childhood, at the contrasting accidents
of a great fortune.

In this essay, save for the change of Blakesware to
Blakesmoor, the experience is related without disguise.
But it is not always easy to disengage fact from fiction in
these more personal confessions. Lamb had a love of
mystifying and putting his readers on a false scent. And
the difficulty of getting at the truth is the greater because

Marvell on Appleton House, to the Lord Fairfax.

he is often most outspoken when we should expect him to
be reticent, and on the other hand alters names and places
when there would seem to be little reason for it.   A
curious instance of this habit is supplied by the touching
reverie called *Dream Children.* This essay appeared in the
London for January, 1822.   Lamb's elder brother John
was then lately dead.   A letter to Wordsworth, of March
in this year, mentions his death as recent, and speaks of a
certain "deadness to everything," which the writer dated
from that event.   The "broad, burly, jovial" John Lamb
(so Talfourd describes him), had lived his own, easy,
prosperous life up to this time, not altogether avoiding
social relations with his brother and sister, but evidently
absorbed to the last in his own interests and pleasures.
The death of this brother, wholly unsympathetic as he was
with Charles, served to bring home to him his loneliness.
He was left in the world with but one near relation, and
that one too often removed from him for months at a time
by the saddest of afflictions.   No wonder if he became
keenly aware of his solitude.   No wonder if his thoughts
turned to what *might* have been, and he looked back to
those boyish days when he wandered in the glades of
Blakesware with Alice by his side.   He imagines himself
with his little ones, who have crept round him to hear
stories about their "great-grandmother Field."   For no
reason that is apparent, while he retains his grandmother's
real name, he places the house in Norfolk, but all the
details that follow are drawn from Blakesware.   "Then I
went on to say how religious and how good their great-
grandmother Field was, how beloved and respected by everybody, though she was not indeed the mistress of this great
house, but had only the charge of it (and yet in some
respects she might be said to be the mistress of it too)

committed to her by its owner, who preferred living in a
newer and more fashionable mansion which he had purchased somewhere in an adjoining county;[2] but still
she lived in it in a manner as if it had been her own,
and kept up the dignity of the great house in a sort while
she lived, which afterwards came to decay, and was nearly
pulled down, and all its old ornaments stripped and carried
away to the owner's other house, where they were set up,
and looked as awkward as if some one were to carry away
the old tombs they had seen lately at the abbey and stick
them up in Lady C.'s tawdry gilt drawing-room.   Here
John smiled, as much as to say, 'That would be foolish
indeed.'"

Inexpressibly touching, when we have once learned to
penetrate the thin disguise in which he clothes them, are
the hoarded memories, the tender regrets, which Lamb,
writing by his "lonely hearth," thus ventured to commit
to the uncertain sympathies of the great public.   More
touching still is the almost superhuman sweetness with
which he deals with the character of his lately lost brother.
He had named his little ones after this brother, and after
their "pretty dead mother"—John and Alice.   And there
is something of the magic of genius, unless, indeed, it was
a burst of uncontrollable anguish, in the revelation with
which his dream ends.   He kept still, as always, the
secret of his beloved's name.   But he tells us who it was
that won the prize from him, and it is no secret that in
this case the real name is given.   The conclusion of this
essay must be our last extract, but it would be difficult to
find one more worthy :—

Then in somewhat a more heightened tone, I told how, though

_____

[2] This is, of course, Gilston, the other seat of the Plumer family.

their great-grandmother Field loved all her grandchildren, yet
in an especial manner she might be said to love their uncle,
John L——, because he was so handsome and spirited a youth,
and a king to the rest of us ; and instead of moping about in
solitary corners, like some of us, he would mount the most
mettlesome horse he could get, when but an imp no bigger than
themselves, and make it carry him half over the county in a morning, and join the hunters when there were any out; and yet he
loved the old house and gardens too, but had too much spirit to
be always pent up within their boundaries ; and how their uncle
grew up to man's estate as brave as he was handsome, to the
admiration of everybody, but of their great-grandmother Field
most especially ; and how he used to carry me upon his back
when I was a lame-footed boy—for he was a good bit older than
me—many a mile when I could not walk for pain ; and how in
after-life he became lame-footed too, and I did not always (I
fear) make allowance enough for him when he was impatient
and in pain, nor remember sufficiently how considerate he had
been to me when I was lame-footed ; and how when he died,
though he had not been dead an hour, it seemed as if he had
died a great while ago, such a distance there is betwixt life and
death ; and how I bore his death as I thought pretty well at
first, but afterwards it haunted and haunted me ; and though I
did not cry or take it to heart as some do, and as I think he
would have done if I had died, yet I missed him all day long
and knew not till then how much I had loved him.   I missed
his kindness and I missed his crossness, and wished him to be
alive again to be quarrelling with him (for we quarrelled sometimes), rather than not have him again, and was as uneasy without him as he their poor uncle must have been when the doctor
took off his limb.   Here the children fell a-crying, and asked if
their little mourning which they had on was not for Uncle John,
and they looked up and prayed me not to go on about their
uncle, but to tell them some stories about their pretty dead
mother.   Then I told how for seven long years, in hope sometimes
sometimes in despair, yet persisting ever, I courted the fair Alice
W——n ; and as much as children could understand, I explained

to them what coyness and difficulty and denial meant in maidens
—when suddenly, turning to Alice, the soul of the first Alice
looked out at her eyes with such a reality of representment, that
I became in doubt which of them stood there before me, or
whose that bright hair was; and while I stood gazing, both
the children gradually grew fainter to my view, receding, and
still receding till nothing at last but two mournful features were
seen in the uttermost distance, which, without speech, strangely
impressed upon me the effects of speech: "We are not of Alice,
nor of thee, nor are we children at all. The children of Alice
call Bartram father. We are nothing; less than nothing, and
dreams. We are only what might have been, and must wait
upon the tedious shores of Lethe millions of ages before we have
existence and a name"—and immediately awaking I found myself quietly seated in my bachelor arm-chair, where I had fallen
asleep, with the faithful Bridget unchanged by my side; but
John L. (or James Elia) was gone for ever.

The space available for quotation is exhausted, and
many sides of Lamb's peculiar faculty are still unre-
presented. Those who have yet to make his acquaintance may be advised to read, in addition to those already
named, the essay *On Some of the Old Actors*, containing
the analysis of the character of Malvolio, a noble example
of the uses which Shakespearian criticism may be made to
serve—the extract from a letter to his friend Barron Field,
a judge in New South Wales, entitled, *Distant Corre-
spondents*, and that called *The Praise of Chimney Sweepers*.
Belonging to the *personal* group, which includes *Blakesmoor* and *Dream Children*, is the paper *Mackery End in
Hertfordshire*, scarcely less delightful. The two critical
essays on Sidney and Wither (the latter, however, does
not belong to the Elia series), contain some of Lamb's
most subtle criticism and most eloquent writing. *Barbara S.* is an anecdote of Fanny Kelly's early life;

and *Captain Jackson* is a character-sketch, which,
despite the vast difference between the two writers,
curiously suggests the fine hand of Miss Austen. Lastly,
the paper with the startling title, *Confessions of a Drunkard*,
is not to be overlooked. A strange interest attaches to this
paper. It had been originally written by Lamb, at the
request of a friend, as one of a series of Temperance Tracts.
In this capacity it had been quoted in an article in the
Quarterly, for April, 1822, as "a fearful picture of the
consequences of intemperance," which the reviewer went
on to say "we have reason to know is a true tale." In
order to give the author the opportunity of contradicting
this statement, the tract was reprinted in the *London* in
the following August, under the signature of Elia. To it
were appended a few words of remonstrance with the
Quarterly reviewer for assuming the literal truthfulness
of these confessions, but accompanied with certain significant admissions that showed Lamb had no right to be
seriously indignant. "It is indeed," he writes, "a compound extracted out of his long observations of the effects
of drinking upon all the world about him; and this
accumulated mass of misery he hath centred (as the
custom is with judicious essayists) in a single figure.
We deny not that a portion of his own experiences may
have passed into the picture (as who, that is not a washy
fellow, but must at some time have felt the after-operation
of a too generous cup?); but then how heightened! how
exaggerated! how little within the sense of the Review,
where a part, in their slanderous usage, must be understood to stand for the whole." The truth is that Lamb
in writing his tract had been playing with edge-tools, and
could hardly have complained if they turned against himself. It would be those who knew Lamb, or at least

the circumstances of his life, best, who would be most
likely to accept these confessions as true. For in the
course of them he gives with curious fidelity the outline
of an experience that was certainly not imaginary. The
' friendly harpies " who came about him for his gin-and-
water, and made its consumption more and more a habit ;
the exchange of these in due course for companions of a
better type, " of intrinsic and felt worth ;" the substitution
for a while, under the influence of two of these, of the
" sweet enemy " tobacco, and the new slavery to this
counter-attraction ; the increasing need of stimulant to
set his wits to work, and the buffoonery indulged under
its effects ; all this is told in a way that no friend of
Lamb could affect to mistake. No doubt the exaggeration
which Lamb pleads is there also, and the drunkard's
utter collapse and misery are described in a style which, as
applied to himself, was absurd. But to call the insinua-
tion that the tract had in it biographic truth, " malig-
nant," as some of Lamb's apologists have done, is not less
absurd. The essay has enough reality in it to live as a
very powerful plea for the virtue of self-restraint, and it
may continue to do good service in the cause.

De Quincey has observed that one chief pleasure we
derive from Lamb's writing is due to a secret satisfaction
in feeling that his admirers must always of necessity be a
select few. There is an unpleasantly cynical flavour about
the remark, but at the same time one understands to what it
points. Thoroughly to understand and enjoy Charles Lamb,
one must have come to entertain a feeling towards him
almost like personal affection, and such a circle of intimates
will always be small. It is necessary to come to the study
of his writings in entire trustfulness, and having first cast
away all prejudice. The reader must be content to enjoy

what is set before him, and not to grumble because any
chance incident on the road tempts the writer away from
the path on which he set out.   If an Essay is headed
Oxford in the Vacation, he must not complain that only half
the paper touches on Oxford, and that the rest is divided
between the writer Elia, and a certain absent-minded old
scholar, George Dyer, on whose peculiarities Lamb was
never weary of dwelling. What, then, is the compensating
charm ?   What is there in these rambling and multi-
farious meditations that proves so stimulating and suggestive ?   There is an epithet commonly applied to Lamb so
hackneyed that one shrinks from using it once more—the
epithet "delightful." No other word certainly seems
more appropriate, and it is perhaps because (in defiance of
etymology) the sound of it suggests that double virtue of
illuminating, and making happy.   It is in vain to attempt
to convey an idea of the impression left by Lamb's style.
It evades analysis.   One might as well seek to account for
the perfume of lavender, or the flavour of quince.   It
is in truth an essence, prepared from flowers and herbs
gathered in fields where the ordinary reader does not
often range.   And the nature of the writer—the alembic
in which these various simples were distilled—was as rare
for sweetness and purity as the best of those enshrined in
the old folios—his "midnight darlings." If he had by
nature the delicate grace of Marvell, and the quaint fancy
of Quarles, he also shared the chivalry of Sidney, and could
lay on himself "the lowliest duties," in the spirit of his best-
beloved of all, John Milton.   It is the man, Charles
Lamb, that constitutes the enduring charm of his written
words. He is, as I have said, an egotist—but an egotist
without a touch of vanity or self-assertion—an egotist
without a grain of envy or ill-nature.   When asked one

day whether he did not hate some person under discus
sion, he retorted, " How could I hate him ? Don't I
know him ?   I never could hate any one I knew."   It is
this humanity that gives to his intellect its flexibility and
its deep vision, that is the feeder at once of his pathos and
his humour.

CHAPTER VII.

THE last six years of Lamb's life, though the most remarkable in his literary annals, had not been fruitful in
incident. The death of his elder brother, already mentioned, was the one event that nearly touched his heart
and spirits. Its effect had been, with the loss of some
other friends about the same time, to produce, he said,
" a certain deadness to everything." It had brought home
to him his loneliness, and moreover served to increase a
long felt weariness of the monotony of office life. Already,
in the beginning of 1822, he was telling Wordsworth, " I
grow ominously tired of official confinement. Thirty years
have I served the Philistines, and my neck is not subdued
to the yoke. You don't know how wearisome it is to
breathe the air of four pent walls, without relief, day after
day, all the golden hours of the day between ten and
four, without ease or interposition. *Tædet me harum
quotidianarum formarum*, these pestilential clerk-faces
always in one's dish. . . . . I dare not whisper to myself
a pension on this side of absolute incapacitation and
infirmity, till years have sucked me dry—*otium cum
indignitate*. I had thought in a green old age (O green

thought!) to have retired to Ponder's End, emblematic
name, how beautiful! in the Ware Road, there to have made
up my accounts with heaven and the Company, toddling
about it between it and Cheshunt, anon stretching, on some
fine Isaac Walton morning, to Hoddesden or Amwell,
careless as a beggar; but walking, walking ever till I
fairly walked myself off my legs, dying walking! The
hope is gone. I sit like Philomel all day (but not singing)
with my heart against this thorn of a desk." Very
touching, by the side of the delightful suggestion of
Ponder's End, is the dream of retirement to the Ware
Road—the road, that is to say, that led to Widford and
Blakesware. If these were not to him exactly what
Auburn was to Goldsmith, he still at times had hopes,—

> His long vexation past,
> There to return, and die at home at last.

Three years were, however, to elapse before he was
at liberty to choose his own place of residence. It is
significant that though he could never bring himself to
live quite beyond reach of town, and the "sweet security
of streets," it was in the Hertfordshire direction that he
turned in his last days, and died as it were half-way
between London and that quiet Hertfordshire village, the
two places he loved best on earth.

There was one incident in those Russell Street days that
would have been an event indeed in the life of most
home-keeping men who had reached middle life without
having once left English shores. In the summer holiday
of 1822 Charles and his sister made a trip to Paris. At
whose suggestion, or in obedience to what sudden impulse,
they were led to make so violent a change in their usual
habits, there is nothing to show. They left England in

the middle of June, and two months later we find Mary
Lamb still in Paris, and seeing the sights under the
direction of their friend, Crabb Robinson. Charles, who
had returned earlier to England, had left a characteristic
note of instructions for his sister's guidance, advising her
to walk along the " Borough side of the Seine," where
she would find a mile and a half of print-shops and bookstalls. " Then," he adds, not unfairly describing a first
impression of Père-la-Chaise, " there is a place where the
Paris people put all their dead people, and bring them
flowers and dolls and gingerbread-nuts and sonnets and
such trifles ; and that is all, I think, worth seeing as
sights, except that the streets and shops of Paris are
themselves the best sight." In a note to Barron Field on
his return, he adds a few more of his experiences, how he
had eaten frogs, fricasseed, " the nicest little delicate
things," and how the Seine was " exactly the size to
run through a magnificent street."

He finds time, however, to add to his hasty note the
pleasant intelligence that he had met Talma. Kenney,
the dramatist, was at this time living at Versailles, and to
him Lamb owed this introduction. Talma had lately
given a thousand francs for what he was assured was an
authentic portrait of Shakespeare, and he invited Kenney
to bring Lamb to see it. " It is painted," Lamb writes, " on
the one half of a pair of bellows, a lovely picture, corresponding with the folio head." It is hard to believe that
Lamb had any doubts about the spuriousness of this relic,
though his language on the point is dubious. He quotes
the rhymes " in old carved wooden letters " that surrounded
the portrait, and adds the significant remark that Ireland
was not found out by his parchments, but by his poetry.
And perhaps he did not wish to hurt Talma's feelings. It

was arranged that the party should see the tragedian in
Regulus the same evening, and that he should sup with
them after the performance.   Lamb, we are told, " could
not at all enter into the spirit of French acting, and in
his general distaste made no exception in favour of his
intended guest.   This, however, did not prevent their
mutual and high relish of each other's character and conversation, nor was any allusion made to the performance,
till, on rising to go, Talma inquired how he liked it.
Lamb shook his head and smiled. 'Ah!' said Talma.
'I was not very happy to-night: you must see me in
Sylla.' 'Incidit in Scyllam,' said Lamb, 'qui vult
vitare Charybdim.'   'Ah! you are a rogue; you are a
great rogue,' said Talma, shaking him cordially by the
hand, as they parted."

There is a sad story, only too likely to be true, that
Mary Lamb was seized with one of her old attacks on the
journey, and had to be left at Amiens in charge of her
attendant.   If so, it may account for her brother avoiding
the subject in later essays and letters.   An Elia essay
embodying even the surface impressions of a month's stay
in Paris would have been a welcome addition to the
number.   Lamb was usually prompt to seize on the latest
incident in his life and turn it to this purpose.   When
short-sighted George Dyer, leaving the cottage at Islington,
walked straight into the New River in broad daylight, the
adventure appears the very next month in the *London
Magazine*, under the heading of *Amicus Redivivus*.   But
France and the French do not seem to have opened any
new vein of humour or observation.   In truth, Lamb
was unused to let his sympathies go forth save in
certain customary directions.   Any persons, and any
book that he had come to know well—any one of the " old

familiar faces "—served to draw out those sympathies. But novelties he almost always passed by unmoved.

The first series of Lamb's essays, under the title of " *Elia* —*Essays that have appeared under that signature in the London Magazine*—was published in a single volume by Taylor and Hessey at the opening of the year 1823. It contained the contributions of something less than two years. As yet there was assuredly no sign of failing power in the brain and heart that produced them. Nor did Lamb cease to contribute to the magazine and elsewhere after the appearance of the first volume. The second series, published ten years later, is an exception to the rule that sequels must necessarily be failures. *Old China* and *Poor Relations*, the *Old Margate Hoy, Blakesmoor, Barbara S.*, and the *Superannuated Man*, which are found in the second series, exhibit all Lamb's qualities at their highest. It was perhaps only a passing mood of melancholy that made him write to Bernard Barton, in March, 1823, when the book had already begun to make its mark—" They have dragged me again into the magazine, but I feel the spirit of the thing in my own mind quite gone. 'Some brains' (I think Ben Jonson says it) 'will endure but one skimming.' " But another cause for this depression may have been at work. There was a painful incident connected with the *Elia* volume from the first, for which even the quick appreciation of the public could not compensate. There had been one exception to the welcome with which the book had been greeted. A word of grave disapprobation, or what had seemed such to Lamb, had been heard amid the chorus of approval, and this word had been spoken by a dear and valued friend.

In the *Quarterly Review* of January, 1823, appeared an

article, known to be by Southey, professing to be a review
of a work by Gregoire, ex-Bishop of Blois, on the rise
and progress of Deism in France. After the fashion of
reviewers, Southey had made the book an occasion for a
general survey of the progress of free thought in England
as well as abroad, and the article was issued with the
alarming title, *Progress of Infidelity.* Towards its close
Southey is led very characteristically into many general
reflections on the reasonableness of belief, and the un-
reasonableness of scepticism, and while engaged on this
line of thought, it seems to have occurred to him that he
might at once "point a moral" and call attention to a friend's
book, by a quotation from the then newly published
volume of Lamb. And this is how he set about it :—

   " Unbelievers have not always been honest enough thus
to express their real feelings ; but this we know concerning them, that when they have renounced their birthright
of hope, they have not been able to divest themselves of
fear. From the nature of the human mind this might be
presumed, and in fact it is so. They may deaden the
heart and stupefy the conscience, but they cannot destroy
the imaginative faculty. There is a remarkable proof of
this in *Elia's Essays,* a book which wants only a sounder
religious feeling, to be as delightful as it is original. In
that upon *Witches and other Night Fears,* he says ' It
is not book or picture, or the stories of foolish servants,
which create these terrors in children. They can at most
but give them a direction. Dear little T. H., who of all
children has been brought up with the most scrupulous
exclusion of every taint of superstition, who was never
allowed to hear of goblin or apparition, or scarcely to be
told of bad men, or to hear or read of any distressing
story, finds all this world of fear, from which he has been

so rigidly exċluded *ab extra*, in his own "thick-coming fancies;" and from his little midnight pillow this nurse-child of optimism will start at shapes, unborrowed of tradition, in sweats to which the reveries of the cell-damned murderer are tranquillity.' "

I have had occasion to refer to this essay before, in speaking of Lamb's childhood. For, as usual, it originated in his own experience. He was led to relate how from the age of four to seven his nightly sleep had been disturbed by childish terrors, in which the grim picture of Saul and the Witch, in Stackhouse's *History of the Bible* had borne so prominent a part. And then, in order to strengthen his argument that these terrors are nervous, and not to be traced to any gloomy or improper religious training, he cites the parallel case, within his own knowledge, of "dear little T. H." All Lamb's friends and associates knew that this was little Thornton Hunt, Leigh Hunt's eldest son. The use of initials was really no disguise at all. Lamb admitted in his subsequent remonstrance with Southey that to call him T. H. was "as good as naming him." If the sanctity of private life had been violated, it was certainly Lamb who had set the example. But, as certainly, he had said nothing to the discredit of the poor child or his parents. According to the ethics of journalism current sixty years ago there was nothing uncommon in this way of indicating living people. Lamb was specially fond of bringing in his friends and acquaintances by their initials. His own family, Coleridge, Norris, Barron Field, and many others, occur repeatedly in his writings in this guise. He was intimate with Leigh Hunt and his young family, and sincerely attached to them. Nothing had been further from his thoughts than to cast any kind of slight upon the little boy, "Thornton Hunt, my favourite

child," or his educators. It must therefore have been
with something more than disgust that he found the
Quarterly Reviewer, proceeding, after the passage just
cited, to point out with unmistakable *animus* that such
nervous terrors were easily to be accounted for in the
case of one who had been brought up in ignorance of all
the facts and consolations of the Christian religion.

It is possible that this gratuitous attack upon a
political opponent, through his own child, was not
added to the article until after it had left Southey's
hands. All that we know from Southey himself is that
his sole object in mentioning Lamb's volume had been to
call attention to its general merits—that he had in the
first instance written "a *saner* religious feeling," which was
the word that exactly expressed his meaning; that happily
remembering in time the previous history of the Lamb
family, he had hastily changed the word to "sounder,"
meaning to re-cast the sentence when the article returned
to him in proof, and that the opportunity never came.
We may be sure that this explanation represents the
whole truth. Southey had written to his friend Wynn,
in the very month in which the article appeared—"Read
Elia, if the book has not fallen in your way. It is by
my old friend, Charles Lamb. There are some things in
it which will offend, and some which will pain you, as
they do me; but you will find in it a rich vein of pure
gold." And the things which pained him were certainly
of a kind about which the word *sane* might be more properly used than the word *sound*. Lamb was probably
mistaken in thinking that Southey referred to certain
familiarities, if not flippancies, of expression on serious
subjects that he may at times have indulged in. On this
score he had a fair retort ready in the various ballads of

diablerie that Southey had not disdained to write, and to publish. Nor was Southey, we may be sure, offended by so genuinely earnest a plea for temperance and rational gratitude as is contained in the essay *Grace before Meat*. Rather (as Lamb evidently suspected) was it such a vein of speculation as that followed out in *New Year's Eve*, which would cause a strange chill to the simple faith and steadfast hopefulness of his friend. As I have said, Lamb seems in this essay to have written with the express purpose of presenting the reverse side of a passage in his favourite *Religio Medici*. Sir Thomas Browne had there written—" I thank God I have not those strait ligaments, or narrow obligations to the world, as to dote on life, or be convulsed and tremble at the name of death." " When I take a full view and circle of my-self without this reasonable moderator, and equal piece of justice, death, I do conceive myself the miserablest person extant." Lamb may have argued (in the very words applied to this treatise in the essay on *Imperfect Sympathies*) that it was all very well for the author of the *Religio Medici*, "mounted upon the airy stilts of abstrac-tion" to "overlook the impertinent individualities of such poor concretions as mankind," but that to him, Elia, death meant something by no means to be defined as a "reason-able moderator," and "equal piece of justice." He clung to the things he saw and loved—the friends, the books, the streets and crowds around him, and he was not ashamed to confess that death meant for him the absence of all these, and that he could not look it steadfastly in the face.

It is worth noticing that the profound melancholy of this essay had already attracted attention, and formed the subject of a copy of verses, in the form of a *Poetical*

Epistle to Elia, signed "Olen," in the *London Magazine*
for August, 1821. Elia had been there taken to task, in
lines of much eloquence and feeling, for his negative
views on the subject of a future life. And indeed, for all
the dallying with paradox, and the free blending of fact
with fiction, in this singular paper, the fragments of personal confession are very remarkable. There are few
things in literature more pathetic than the contrast drawn
between the two stages of his own life, as if he would
have given the lie sadly to his friend's adage about the
child being father of the man :—

If I know aught of myself, no one whose mind is intro-
spective—and mine is painfully so—can have a less respect for
his present identity, than I have for the man Elia. I know him
to be light, and vain, and humoursome; a notorious . . . . ;
addicted to . . . . ; averse from counsel, neither taking it nor
offering it; . . . . besides; a stammering buffoon; what you
will; lay it on, and spare not; I subscribe to it all, and much
more than thou canst be willing to lay at his door—but for the
child Elia—that "other me" there in the background—I must
take leave to cherish the remembrance of that young master,
with as little reference, I protest, to this stupid changeling of
five-and-forty as if it had been a child of some other house, and
not of my parents. I can cry over its patient small-pox at five,
and rougher medicaments. I can lay its poor fevered head
upon the sick pillow at Christ's, and wake with it in surprise at
the gentle posture of maternal tenderness hanging over it, that
unknown had watched its sleep. I know how it shrank from
any the least colour of falsehood. God help thee, Elia, how art
thou changed! Thou art sophisticated. I know how honest,
how courageous (for a weakling) it was; how religious, how
imaginative, how hopeful! From what have I not fallen if the
child I remember was indeed myself, and not some dissembling
guardian, presenting a false identity, to give the rule to my
unpractised steps, and regulate the tone of my moral being.

Although the gloom is relieved by no ray of hope or consolation, the reality of the self-reproach might well have saved the writer from criticism, even as to the "sanity" of his religious feeling.

Lamb was annoyed, rather than deeply hurt, by the attack upon himself. He had old grievances against the *Quarterly Review.* Eight or nine years before, he had written for it a review of Wordsworth's *Excursion,* which Gifford inserted after alterations that Lamb compared to pulling out the eyes and leaving only the bleeding sockets. "I cannot give you an idea of what he (Gifford) has done to it," he wrote to Wordsworth. " The *language* he has altered throughout. Whatever inadequateness it had to its subject, it was, in point of composition, the prettiest piece of prose I ever writ." And it is clear from the article itself, as it appears in the number for October, 1814, that this language is not exaggerated. The sweetness and delicate perception of the author are there, but the diction bears little of his peculiar mark. Then had come the unfortunate reference to the *Confessions of a Drunkard,* already mentioned. In general the *Quarterly* set were in implacable opposition to the Lamb set, and now, not for the first time, he had to hear hard things said, not only of himself, but of those who were bound to him by ties of strong affection. He seems not to have been informed of the attack till some months after its appearance. It is not till the July following, at least, that any mention of it occurs in his letters. In that month he writes to Bernard Barton, " Southey has attacked *Elia* on the score of infidelity, in the *Quarterly* article, *Progress of Infidelity.* He might have spared an old friend such a construction of a few careless flights, that meant no harm to religion. If all *his* unguarded expressions on the

subject were to be collected—but I love and respect
Southey, and will not retort. I hate his review and his
being a reviewer. The hint he has dropped will knock
the sale of the book on the head, which was almost at a
stop before." This last apprehension was evidently
groundless. There is no reason to suppose that the book
made its way more slowly for the paragraph in the
review. For whatever here and there is morbid in them,
the *Essays* themselves contain the best antidote.

Lamb could not resist the opportunity it afforded him
for a fresh essay of Elia, and in the *London* for October,
1823, appeared the *Letter of Elia to Robert Southey,
Esq.* As a whole, it is not one of Lamb's happiest
efforts. His more valid grounds of complaint against the
review are set forth with sufficient dignity and force. He
urges quite fairly that to say a book " wants a sounder
religious feeling," is to say either too much or too little.
And the indecency of attacking Leigh Hunt through his
own child, a boy of twelve, is properly rebuked. But
when Lamb carries the war into the enemy's territory, he
is less successful. As two blacks do not make a white, it
was beside the mark to make laborious fun over Southey's
youthful ballads ; and the grievance as to the fees extorted
from visitors to Westminster Abbey comes in rather flatly
as a peroration. The concluding paragraphs of the letter
are the only portions that Lamb afterwards thought well
to reprint. They appeared, ten years later, in the Second
Series of *Elia* under the title of *Tombs of the Abbey.* The
letter, as a whole, is given in Talfourd's Memorials.

Lamb was not so deeply moved by Southey's criticism
but that he could make some sport over his annoyance.
What actually galled him was the attack, through himself,
upon a friend. In previous articles in the same Review

he had found himself complimented at the expense of
another friend, William Hazlitt. And now he took the
opportunity to vindicate his friendship for both Hunt and
Hazlitt in a passage that forms the most interesting and
valuable portion of the letter. There had been a coolness,
he tells us, between himself and Hazlitt, and it is pleasant
to know that Lamb's generosity of tone at this time helped
to make the relations between them once more cordial.
" Protesting," he says, " against much that he has written,
and some things which he chooses to do ; judging him by
his conversation which I enjoyed so long, and relished so
deeply ; or by his books, in those places where no clouding
passion intervenes, I should belie my own conscience
if I said less than that I think W. H. to be, in his
natural and healthy state, one of the wisest and finest
spirits breathing. So far from being ashamed of that
intimacy which was betwixt us, it is my boast that I was
able for so many years to have preserved it entire ; and I
think I shall go to my grave without finding or expecting
to find such another companion." Not less manly and
noble is the justification of his steady friendship for Leigh
Hunt, at that time living abroad, and with a reputation in
England of ill savour with those to whom the pages of the
Quarterly were addressed. " L. H. is now in Italy ; on
his departure to which land, with much regret, I took
my leave of him and of his little family, seven of them, sir,
with their mother, and as kind a set of little people (T. H
and all), as affectionate children as ever blessed a parent.
Had you seen them, sir, I think you could not have looked
upon them as so many little Jonases, but rather as pledges
of the vessel's safety, that was to bear such a freight of
love. I wish you would read Mr. H.'s lines to that
same T. H., " six years old, during a sickness,"—

Sleep breaks at last from out thee,
My little patient boy—

(they are to be found on the 47th page of *Foliage*)—and
ask yourself how far they are out of the spirit of
Christianity."

As he wrote these words, Lamb may have recalled how
his own unfailing sympathy had been a comfort to this
friend in those darker days when Leigh Hunt was undergoing his two years' imprisonment in the Surrey jail
for his newspaper attack on the Prince Regent. Lamb
and his sister were among the Hunts' most regular
visitors at that time. "My eldest little boy," writes
Hunt in his *Autobiography*, "was my constant companion,
and we used to play all sorts of juvenile games together."
And it was on watching the child at play among the
uncongenial surroundings of prison life that Lamb had
written his own lines to "T. L. H.—a child," comforting
child and father with the thought that the time of
deliverance was at hand, when the boy would be once
more in his native element, breathing the healthful air
and plucking the wild flowers on Hampstead Heath.
Lamb was always tender over children, and these lines
have a simplicity, over and above their studied quaintness,
that savours pleasantly of Blake :—

Guileless traitor, rebel mild,
Convict unconscious, culprit-child !
Gates that close with iron roar
Have been to thee thy nursery door:
Chains that chink in cheerless cells
Have been thy rattles and thy bells :
Walls contrived for giant sin
Have hemmed thy faultless weakness in :
Near thy sinless bed black guilt
Her discordant house hath built,

And filled it with her monstrous brood—
Sights by thee not understood—
Sights of fear, and of distress,
That pass a harmless infant's guess !
But the clouds that overcast
Thy young morning, may not last.
Soon shall arrive the rescuing hour
That yields thee up to Nature's power.
Nature that so late doth greet thee
Shall in o'erflowing measure meet thee.
She shall recompense with cost
For every lesson thou hast lost.
Then wandering up thy sire's loved hill
Thou shalt take thy airy fill
Of health and pastime. *Birds shall sing
For thy delight each May morning.*
'Mid new-yeaned lambkins thou shalt play,
Hardly less a lamb than they.
Then thy prison's lengthened bound
Shall be the horizon skirting round.
And, while thou fill'st thy lap with flowers
To make amends for wintry hours,
The breeze, the sunshine, and the place,
Shall from thy tender brow efface
Each vestige of untimely care
That sour restraint had graven there ;
And on thy every look impress
A more excelling childishness.
So shall be thy days beguiled,
Thornton Hunt, my favourite child.

Southey first learned from the pages of the *London
Magazine* the effect of the language used by him in the
Quarterly Review. " On my part," he wrote to his publisher, after reading Lamb's epistle, " there was not even a
momentary feeling of anger. I was very much surprised
and grieved, because I knew how much he would condemn
himself, and yet no resentful letter was ever written less
offensively ; his gentle nature may be seen in it through-

out." Southey was in London in the month after the
publication of Lamb's remonstrance, and wrote him a letter
in language full of affection and sorrow. The soreness at
once passed away. "Dear Southey," he replied, "the
kindness of your note has melted away the mist which was
upon me. I have been fighting against a shadow. That
accursed *Q. R.* had vexed me by a gratuitous speaking, of
its own knowledge, that the *Confessions of a D——d*
was a genuine description of the state of the writer. Little
things that are not ill meant may produce much ill. *That*
might have injured me alive and dead : I am in a public
office, and my life is insured. I was prepared for anger,
and I thought I saw in a few obnoxious words a hard
case of repetition directed against me. I wish both Magazine and Review at the bottom of the sea. I shall be
ashamed to see you, and my sister (though innocent) still
more so ; for the folly was done without her knowledge,
and has made her uneasy ever since. My guardian angel
was absent at that time. I will muster up courage to see
you, however, any day next week. We shall hope that
you will bring Edith with you. That will be a second
mortification. She will hate to see us; but come, and heap
embers. We deserve it—I for what I've done, and she
for being my sister." The visit was paid, and the old
intimacy renewed, never again to be weakened by unkindly
word.

In this note to Southey, Lamb has to tell of a change of
address. In August of this year he and his sister had
finally moved from Russell Street, and for the first time in
their united lives became householders. The rooms over
the brazier's had from the first had many drawbacks, and
for some years the brother and sister had occasionally retired to a rural lodging at Dalston, partly to enjoy a short

respite from the din of the theatres and the market, but
chiefly that Charles might be able to write without interruption from the increasing band of intruders on his scanty
leisure. There is a pretty glimpse of one such period of
retreat in a note to Miss Hutchinson of April in this
year—" Meanwhile of afternoons we pick up primroses at
Dalston, and Mary corrects me when I call 'em cowslips."
And now they resolved to fix their tent permanently
within reach of primroses and cowslips, and Charles
must tell the story in his own words. He writes
to Bernard Barton :—" When you come Londonward,
you will find me no longer in Covent Garden. I
have a cottage in Colebrook Row, Islington ; a cottage,
for it is detached ; a white house with six good rooms ;
the New River (rather elderly by this time) runs (if a
moderate walking pace can be so termed) close to the foot
of the house ; and behind is a spacious garden with vines
(I assure you), pears, strawberries, parsnips, leeks, carrots,
cabbages, to delight the heart of old Alcinous. You enter
without passage into a cheerful dining-room, all studded
over and rough with old books ; and above is a lightsome
drawing-room, three windows, full of choice prints. I feel
like a great lord, never having had a house before." The
sequel must be given, so amusingly illustrative of the
snares and pitfalls that are inseparable even from rural
felicity :—" I am so taken up with pruning and gardening,
quite a new sort of occupation to me. I have gathered
my Jargonels, but my Windsor pears are backward. The
former were of exquisite raciness. I do now sit under my
own vine and contemplate the growth of vegetable nature.
I can now understand in what sense they speak of father
Adam. I recognize the paternity while I watch my tulips.
I almost fell with him, for the first day I turned a drunken

gardener (as he let in the serpent) into my Eden, and he laid about him, lopping off some choice boughs, &c., which hung over from a neighbour's garden, and in his blind zeal laid waste a shade which had sheltered their window from the gaze of passers-by. The old gentlewoman (fury made her not handsome) could scarcely be reconciled by all my fine words. There was no buttering her parsnips. She talked of the law. What a lapse to commit on the first day of my happy ' garden state ' ! "

The same letter tells of the failing fortunes of the *London Magazine.* Lamb was still contributing to its pages, though not so regularly as of old. He speaks of himself as lingering among its creaking rafters, like the last rat, and of many ominous secessions from the ranks of its old supporters. Hazlitt and Procter had forsaken it, and with them one who might well have been spared before, the wretched Wainwright, who had contributed to its pages various flimsy and conceited rhapsodies on art and letters. It is characteristic of Lamb that he always finds some good-natured word to say of this man, such as " kind " or " light-hearted," principally, no doubt, because the others of his set looked on him with some suspicion. It was his way to seek for the redeeming qualities in those the world looked coldly on. He did not live to know the worst of this now notorious hypocrite and scoundrel.

In their autumn holiday of 1823, Charles and Mary Lamb made an acquaintance destined for the next ten years to add a new and most happy interest to their lonely lives. They were still faithful to the University towns in vacation time, and at the house of a friend in Cambridge, where Charles liked to play his evening game at whist, they found a little girl, the orphan daughter of Charles Isola, one of the Esquire Bedells of the University ; her grandfather, an Italian refugee, having settled in Cambridge as teacher of his own language. The child, who was at other times at school, spent her holidays with an aunt in Cambridge. The Lambs took a strong fancy to her, invited her to stay with them during her next holidays, and finally adopted her. She called them uncle and aunt, and their house was generally her home, until her marriage with Mr. Moxon, the publisher, in 1833. The education of this young girl became the constant care of the brother and sister. They wished to give her the means of becoming herself a teacher, in the event of her not marrying, and while Charles taught her Latin, Mary Lamb worked hard at French that she might assist her young pupil. Many are the allusions in the letters of the last years to "our Emma ;" and as Mary Lamb's periods of mental derangement became more and more frequent and protracted, this new relationship became ever a greater comfort to them both.

In the meantime Charles was fretting under the unbroken confinement of office life. "I have been insuperably dull and lethargic for many weeks," he writes to Bernard Barton early in 1824, "and cannot rise to the vigour of a letter, much léss an essay. The *London* must do without me for a time, for I have lost all interest about it." A subsequent letter, in August, tells the same tale of increasing weariness. "The same indisposition to write has stopped my 'Elias,' but you will see a futile effort in the next number, 'wrung from me with slow pain.' The fact is, my head is seldom cool enough. I am dreadfully indolent." The "futile effort" in the next number was no other than the beautiful essay on *Blakesmoor*, fresh proof (if any were needed) that "difficult writing" need not make itself felt as such by the reader. Nothing more

unforced in style ever came from Charles Lamb's hand—
no sentences more perfect in feeling and expression than
those with which it ends :—

Mine, too—whose else ?—the costly fruit-garden, with its sun-
baked southern wall ; the ampler pleasure-garden, rising backwards from the house in triple terraces, with flower-pots, now of
palest lead, save that a speck, here and there, saved from the
elements, bespoke their pristine state to have been gilt and
glittering ; the verdant quarters, backwarder still ; and, stretching still beyond, in old formality, the firry wilderness, the haunt
of the squirrel and the day-long-murmuring wood-pigeon, with
that antique image in the centre, god or goddess I wist not ;
but child of Athens or old Rome paid never a sincerer worship
to Pan or to Sylvanus in their native groves, than I to that
fragmental mystery.

Was it for this, that I kissed my childish hands too fervently
in your idol worship, walks and windings of Blakesmoor ! for
this, or what sin of mine, has the plough passed over your
pleasant places ? I sometimes think that as men, when they
die, do not die all, so of their extinguished habitations there
may be a hope—a germ to be revivified.

The " firry wilderness " still remains, and in the grassy
meadow where house and garden once stood may faintly be
traced the undulations of the ground where the triple
terraces rose backwards ; but this is all of the actual
Blakesmoor that survives. Yet in this very essay Lamb
has fulfilled his own happy vision, and revivified for all
time that " extinguished habitation."

In spite of indolence and low spirits, the hand of Lamb
had not lost its cunning, as the pretty Album verses
written for Bernard Barton's daughter, Lucy, sufficiently
testify. They were sent to Barton at the end of this
month, September. "I am ill at these numbers," he

pleaded, "but if the above be not too mean to have a place
in thy daughter's sanctum, take them with pleasure." The
lines are interesting, as giving another proof of Lamb's
native sympathy with the Quaker simplicity. His Elia
essay on the *Quakers' Meeting* has shown it. He had
impressed Leigh Hunt, when a boy, by his Quaker-like
demeanour. He had conveyed to Hood, we remember, on
their first meeting, the idea of a " Quaker in black." He
had told Barton in an earlier letter, "In feelings, and
matters not dogmatical, I hope I am half a Quaker." And
here, taking the word *Album* as text, "little book, sur-
named of *White*," he descants on the themes alone fitted
to find shelter in such a home :—

> Whitest thoughts, in whitest dress,
> Candid meanings, best express
> Mind of quiet Quakeress.

In February and March of the following year, his letters
to Barton—the correspondent who now drew forth his best
and most varied powers—show that the desire for rest was
becoming irritably strong. " Your gentleman brother sets
my mouth watering after liberty. Oh that I were kicked
out of Leadenhall with every mark of indignity, and a
competence in my fob. The birds of the air would not be
so free as I should. How I would prance and curvet it,
and pick up cowslips, and ramble about purposeless as an
idiot !" Later in March we learn that he had conveyed
to the Directors of the East India Company his willing-
ness to resign. " I am sick of hope deferred," he writes.
" The grand wheel is in agitation that is to turn up my
fortune ; but round it rolls, and will turn up nothing. I
have a glimpse of freedom, of becoming a gentleman at
large, but I am put off from day to day. I have offered

L

my resignation, and it is neither accepted nor rejected.
Eight weeks am I kept in this fearful suspense. Guess
what an absorbing state I feel it. I am not conscious of
the existence of friends, present or absent. The East
India Directors alone can be that thing to me, or not. I
have just learned that nothing will be decided this week.
Why the next? why any week?"

When he wrote these words, the gratification of his
hopes was nearer than he thought. He can scarcely have
had any serious anxiety as to the result of his application.
Some weeks before he had received some kind of intimation that the matter might be arranged to his satisfaction,
and his medical friends had certified that failing health
and spirits made the step at least desirable. But he had
served only thirty-three years, and it was not unusual for
clerks to complete a term of forty or fifty years' service, so
that he may have had some uneasy doubts as to the
amount of pension. But all doubts were happily dis-
pelled on the last Tuesday in March, 1825, when the
Directors sent for him and acquainted him with the resolution they had passed.

Lamb has described this interview in several letters, but
nowhere so fully as in the Elia essay, the *Superannuated
Man*, which, after his custom, he at once prepared for the
next month s *London Magazine*. With the one exception,
that he transforms the Directors of the India House into a
private firm of merchants, and with one or two other slight
changes of detail, the account seems to be a faithful version of what actually happened.

A week passed in this manner, the most anxious one, I verily
believe, in my life, when on the evening of the 12th of April,
just as I was about quitting my desk to go home (it might be

about eight o'clock) I received an awful summons to attend the presence of the whole assembled firm in the formidable back parlour. I thought, Now my time has surely come; I have done for myself. I am going to be told that they have no longer occasion for me. L——, I could see, smiled at the terror I was in, which was a little relief to me; when to my utter astonishment, B——, the eldest partner, began a formal harangue to me on the length of my services, my very meritorious conduct during the whole of the time (the deuce, thought I, how did he find out that? I protest I never had the confidence to think as much). He went on to descant on the expediency of retiring at a certain time of life (how my heart panted!) and asking me a few questions as to the amount of my own property, of which I have a little, ended with a proposal, to which his three partners nodded a grave assent, that I should accept from the house which I had served so well a pension for life to the amount of two-thirds of my accustomed salary—a magnificent offer! I do not know what I answered between surprise and gratitude, but it was understood that I accepted their proposal, and I was told that I was free from that hour to leave their service. I stammered out a bow, and at just ten minutes after eight I went home—for ever.

The munificence thus recorded was happily no fiction. Lamb's full salary at the time was little short of seven hundred a year, and the offer made to him was a pension of four hundred and fifty, with a deduction of nine pounds a year to secure a fitting provision for his sister, in the event of her surviving him. " Here am I," he writes to Wordsworth, ' after thirty-three years' slavery, sitting in my own room at eleven o'clock, this finest of all April mornings, a freed man, with 441*l.* a year for the remainder of my life, live I as long as John Dennis, who outlived his annuity, and starved at ninety.' "

The East India Directors seem to have been generous

and considerate in a marked degree. If they wished to pay
some compliment to literature in the person of their distinguished clerk, it was not less to their credit. But in
spite of Lamb's modest language as to his official claims
upon their kindness, it would seem that he served them
steadily and faithfully during those thirty-three years.
Save for his brief annual holiday, he stuck to his post. He
wrote his letters from the desk in Leadenhall Street, and
received some of his callers there, but there is nothing to
show that he neglected his daily work. He had sometimes
to tell of headache and indisposition, as when he had been
dining with the poets the night before, where they had
not "quaffed Hippocrene, but Hippocrass rather." And
there is a tradition,—not to be too curiously questioned—
that on occasion of being reproved for coming to the
office late in the mornings, he pleaded that he made up for
it by going away very early. But these peccadilloes are as
nothing set against the long extent of actual service, and
the hearty and spontaneous action of his employers at its
close.

Though Lamb had always fretted against what he called
his slavery to the "desk's dead wood," the discipline of
regular, and even of mechanical work, was of infinite
service to him. With his special temperament, bodily
and mental, he needed, of all men, the compulsion of
duty. The "unchartered freedom" and the "weight of
chance desires," which his friend Wordsworth has so
feelingly lamented, would have been shipwreck to him.
When deliverance from the necessity of toil came, he
could not altogether resist their baneful effects. And we
may be sure that we should not have had more, but fewer
Essays of Elia, if the daily routine of different labour
had been less severe or regular. He was well paid for the

best of his literary work, but there was no pressure upon him to write for bread. "Thank God," he writes to Bernard Barton, "you and I are something besides being writers! There is corn in Egypt, while there is cash at Leadenhall!"

CHAPTER VIII.

(1826—1834.)

" I CAME home FOR EVER on Tuesday in last week," Lamb
writes to Wordsworth, on the 6th of April, 1825.
" The incomprehensibleness of my condition overwhelmed
me. It was like passing from life into eternity. Every
year to be as long as three, i.e., to have three times as
much real time—time that is my own, in it! I wandered
about thinking I was happy, but feeling I was not. But
that tumultuousness is passing off, and I begin to understand the nature of the gift. Holidays, even the annual
month, were always uneasy joys: their conscious fugitive-
ness; the craving after making the most of them. Now,
when all is holiday, there are no holidays. I can sit at
home, in rain or shine, without a restless impulse for
walkings. I am daily steadying, and shall soon find it
as natural to me to be my own master, as it has been irk-
some to have had a master. Mary wakes every morning
with an obscure feeling that some good has happened
to us."

Certain misgivings as to the consequences of the step
he had taken are apparent here, even in his words of
congratulation. They appear elsewhere, as in a letter to
Barton of the same month, where he tells how the day

before he had gone back and sat at his old desk among
his old companions, and felt yearnings at having left
them in the lurch. Still, he was forcing himself to take
the most hopeful view of the change in his life, and the
essay on the *Superannuated Man*, that appeared a month
later in the *London*, elaborates with excellent skill the
feelings which he wished to cultivate and preserve. " A
man can never have too much Time to himself, nor too
little to do. Had I a little son, I would christen him
Nothing-to-do ; he should do nothing. Man, I verily
believe, is out of his element as long as he is operative. I
am altogether for the life contemplative."

One of the earliest uses that he made of his freedom
was to pay visits out of London with Mary. In the
summer they are at Enfield, having quiet holidays.
" Mary walks her twelve miles a day some days," Charles
writes to Southey in August, " and I my twenty on others.
Tis all holiday with me now, you know. The change
works admirably." But as time went on, the change was
found to be less admirable. The spur and the discipline
of regular hours and occupation being taken away, Lamb
had to make occupation, or else to find amusement in its
stead. He had been always fond of walking, and he now
tried the experiment of a companion in his walks in the
shape of a dog, Dash, that Hood had given him. But
the dog proved unmanageable, and was fond of running
away down any other streets than those intended by his
master, and Lamb had to part with him a year or two
later in despair. He passed Dash on to Mr. Patmore,
and to this change of ownership we owe the amusing
letter in which he writes for information as to the dog's
welfare. " Dear P., excuse my anxiety, but how is Dash ?
I should have asked if Mrs. Patmore kept her rules, and

was improving : but Dash came uppermost. The order
of our thought should be the order of our writing. Goes
he muzzled, or *aperto ore ?* Are his intellects sound, or
does he wander a little in *his* conversation ? You cannot
be too careful to watch the first symptoms of incoherence.
The first illogical snarl he makes—to St.Luke's with him.
All the dogs here are going mad, if you can believe the over-
seers : but I protest, they seem to me very rational and
collected. But nothing is so deceitful as mad people, to
those who are not used to them. Try him with hot water ;
if he won't lick it up it is a sign—he does not like it.
Does his tail wag horizontally, or perpendicularly ? That
has decided the fate of many dogs in Enfield. Is his
general deportment cheerful ? I mean when he is pleased,
for otherwise there is no judging. You can't be too
careful. Has he bit any of the children yet ? If he has,
have them shot, and keep *him* for curiosity, to see if it is
the hydrophobia"—and so this "excellent fooling" rambles
on into still wilder extravagances. " We are dawdling
our time away very idly and pleasantly " the letter concludes, " at a Mrs. Leishman's, Chace, Enfield, where if
you come a hunting, we can give you cold meat and a
tankard." For two years from the time of his leaving the
India House, the brother and sister paid occasional visits
to Mrs. Leishman's lodgings, until, finally, in 1827, they
became sole tenants of the little house, furnished.

The year 1827 opened sadly for Charles and Mary Lamb.
Since the death of their father, thirty years before, they
had not had to mourn the loss of many friends connected
with their early life. Their brother John had died five
years before—but he had helped to make their real loneliness felt, rather than to relieve it—and they had no
other near relations. But there was one dear friend

of the family, who had been associated with them in their
seasons of heaviest sorrow and hardest struggle. This was
Mr. Randal Norris, for many years sub-treasurer and
librarian of the Inner Temple, whose name has occurred
so often in Lamb's letters and essays. The families of
Norris and Lamb were united by more than one bond of
friendship. They were neighbours in the Temple for
many years, and Mrs. Norris was a native of Widford, and
a friend of the old housekeeper at Blakesware. And now
Charles writes to Crabb Robinson to tell him that this,
his oldest friend, is dying. "In him I have a loss the
world cannot make up. He was my friend and my
father's friend all the life I can remember. I seem to
have made foolish friendships ever since. These are
friendships which outlive a second generation. Old
as I am waxing, in his eyes I was still the child he
first knew me. To the last he called me Charley.
I have none to call me Charley now. He was the
last link that bound me to the Temple. You are but of
yesterday. In him seem to have died the old plainness of manners and singleness of heart." In a few days
the lingering illness was over, and the old friend was
laid to rest in the Temple Church-yard.

During the year that followed, Lamb found a con-
genial occupation, and a healthy substitute for his old
regular hours, in working daily at the British Museum.
He wished to assist Hone, the editor of the *Every Day
Books*, and undertook to make extracts, on the plan of
his former volumes of Dramatic Specimens, from the
collection of plays bequeathed by Garrick to the
British Museum, for publication in *Hone's Table Book*.
" It is a sort of office-work to me," he writes to
Barton, " hours, ten to four, the same. It does me

good. Man must have regular occupation that has
been used to it." The extracts thus chosen were con-
fessedly but gleanings after the earlier volumes, and
in the scanty comments prefixed to them there is a
corresponding falling off in interest. The remark upon
Gorboduc, that " there may be flesh and blood underneath,
but we cannot get at it " shows the old keenness of observation. And it is pleasant to hear him repeat once more
that the plays of Shakespeare have been the " strongest
and sweetest food of his mind from infancy." But the
real impetus to the study of the great Elizabethans had
been given in the volumes of 1808.

A series of short essays contributed in this same year
to the *New Monthly Magazine,* under the title of *Popular
Fallacies,* are for the most part of slight value. The one
of these that was the author's favourite is suggested by
the saying that " Home is home, though it is never so
homely." The first exception that he propounds to
the truth of this maxim is in the case of the " very poor."
To places of cheap entertainment, and the benches of ale-
houses, Lamb says, the poor man " resorts for an image of
the home which he cannot find at home." Very touching is the picture he goes on to draw of the discrepancy
between the " humble meal shared together," as described
by the sentimentalist, and the grim irony of the actual
facts. " The innocent prattle of his children takes out the
sting of a man's poverty. But the children of the very
poor do not prattle. It is none of the least frightful
features in that condition that there is no childishness in
its dwellings. Poor people, said a sensible nurse to us
once, do not bring up their children, they drag them up."
The whole passage is in a strain of more sustained earnest-
ness than is usual with Lamb, and serves to show how

widely his sympathetic heart had travelled. From this
theme he turns to one which touched his own circumstances more nearly. There is yet another home, he says,
which gives the lie to the popular saying. It may have
all the material comforts that are wanting to the poor man,
all its fire-side conveniences, and yet be *no home*. "It
is the house of the man that is infested with many
visitors." And he goes on to draw the distinction between
the noble-hearted friends that are always welcome, and
the purposeless droppers in at meal-time, or just at the
moment that you have sat down to a book. "They
have a peculiarly compassionating sneer with which they
hope that they do not interrupt your studies." It is
Charles Lamb himself who is here publishing to the
world the old grievance, which appears so constantly
in his letters. He was being driven from Islington by the
crowd of callers and droppers in, from whom he professed
his inability to escape in any other way. Hardly is he
settled at Enfield, in August 1827, when he has to protest
that the swarm of gnats follows him from place to place.
" Whither can I take wing," he writes to Barton "from
the oppression of human faces ? Would I were in a wilderness of apes, tossing cocoa-nuts about, grinning and
grinned at ! "

There is reason to believe, as already observed, that
Lamb was in part responsible for these idle trespassers
upon his time. He had not had the courage to keep
them off when his days were fully occupied, and his
evenings were his only time for literature ; and now,
when he passed for a man wholly at leisure, it was
not likely that the annoyance would diminish. But
the truth is, there was an element of irritability in
Lamb, due to the family temperament, which the

new life, though he could now "wander at his own
sweet will," was little calculated to appease. The rest
of which he dreamed, when he retired in the prime of
life from professional work, could only mean, to such a
temperament as Lamb's, restlessness. He looked for
relief from many troubles in the mere circumstance of
change. It was the *cœlum, non animum* disillusion that
so many have had to experience. And at the same
time he hated having to break with old associations, and
to part from anything to which he had been long accustomed. When he moved to Enfield, in the autumn of
1827, he wrote to Hood that he had had "*no* health" at
Islington, and having found benefit from previous visits
at Enfield, was going to make his abode there altogether.
But, he adds, "'twas with some pain we were evulsed
from Colebrook. To change habitations is to die to
them ; and in my time I have died seven deaths. But I
don't know whether such change does not bring with it
a rejuvenescence. 'Tis an enterprise ; and shoves back the
sense of death's approximating, which though not terrible
to me, is at all times particularly distasteful." The letter
ends in a more cheerful vein, with news of ten pounds a
year less rent than at Islington, and many anticipations of
occasional trips to London " to breathe the fresher air of
the metropolis," and of the curds and cream he and Mary
would set before Hood and Jerdan and other London
friends who might visit them in their country home.
Some of these joys were to be realized, and there are
many signs of the old humour and fancy not having been
altogether banished by the separation from London interests and friends. Mrs. Shelley meets him in town in
August, 1828, and writes to Leigh Hunt, " On my return
to the Strand, I saw Lamb, who was very entertaining

and amiable, though a little deaf.   One of the first questions he asked me was, whether they made puns in Italy.
I said 'Yes, now Hunt is there.'   He said that Burney
made a pun in Otaheite, the first that ever was made in
that country.   At first the natives could not make out
what he meant ; but all at once they discovered the pun,
and danced round him in transports of joy."

Lamb's work in literature was now substantially over,
and he did little more than trifle with it, pleasantly
and ingeniously, for the last few years.   The *London
Magazine*, after a long decay, and many changes of
management, came to an end in 1826 ; and though
some of Lamb's later contributions to the *New Monthly*
and the *Englishman's Magazine* were included in the
Last Essays of Elia, collected and published in 1833,
Elia may be said to have been born, and to have died,
with the *London Magazine*.   In 1828 he wrote, at the
request of the wife of Thomas Hood, who had lately lost
a child, the well-known lines, *On an infant dying as soon
as born*, redolent of the spirit and fancy of Ben Jonson
and the later Elizabethans, and though written to order
showing no lack of spontaneity.   He continued to supply
his young lady friends with acrostics and other such contributions to their albums.   He suffered, as he alleged,
terrible things from albums at this time.   They were
another of the taxes he found ruthlessly exacted from
"retired leisure."   He writes to Procter in 1829 :—

We are in the last ages of the world, when St. Paul prophesied
that women should be " headstrong, lovers of their own wills,
having albums."   I fled hither to escape the albumean perse-
cution, and had not been in my new house twenty-four hours
when the daughter of the next house came in with a friend's
album to beg a contribution, and the following day intimated

she had one of her own. Two more have sprung up since. If
I take the wings of the morning, and fly unto the uttermost
parts of the earth, there will albums be. New Holland has
albums. But the age is to be complied with.

He so far complied with the age as to produce enough,
with a few occasional verses of other kinds, to make a
little volume for his friend Moxon, then newly starting as
a publisher, to issue in appropriate shape, in 1830.

The "new house" spoken of in the letter just quoted
was the Enfield house already mentioned; but in the
summer of 1829 Charles and Mary Lamb again changed
their home. The sister's illnesses were becoming more
frequent and more protracted, and the cares of housekeeping weighed too heavily on her. Their old servant,
Becky, had married and left them, and they were little
contented with her successor. There is a gloomy letter of
Charles to his constant correspondent Barton, in July of
this year, telling how time was *not* lightening the difficulties of a man with no settled occupation. He had
been paying a visit in London, but even London was not
what it had been.

The streets, the shops, are left, but all old friends are gone.
. . . . When I took leave of our adopted young friend at Charing
Cross, 'twas heavy, unfeeling rain, and I had nowhere to go.
Home have I none, and not a sympathizing house to turn to in
the great city. Never did the waters of heaven pour down on a
forlorner head. . . . . I got home on Thursday, convinced that
I was better to get home to my home at Enfield, and hide like a
sick cat in my corner. And to make me more alone, our
ill-tempered maid is gone, who, with all her airs, was yet a
home-piece of furniture, a record of better days; the young
thing that has succeeded her is good and attentive, but she is
nothing. And I have no one here to talk over old matters with.

. . . . What I can do, and do over-do, is to walk ; but deadly
long are the days, these summer all-day days, with but a half-
hour's candle-light and no fire-light. . . . . I pity you for over-
work, but I assure you no work is worse. The mind preys on
itself—the most unwholesome food. I bragged formerly that I
could not have too much time. I have a surfeit. With few
years to come, the days are wearisome. But weariness is not
eternal. Something will shine out to take the load off that flags
me, which is at present intolerable. I have killed an hour or
two in this poor scrawl. I am a sanguinary murderer of time,
and would kill him inch-meal just now. But the snake is vital.
Well, I shall write merrier anon.

A letter of a week or two before had given sadder
reasons for this depression of spirits. Mary Lamb had
again been taken ill, and it had been necessary to remove
her from home.

I have been very desolate indeed. My loneliness is a little
abated by our young friend Emma having just come here for her
holidays, and a schoolfellow of hers that was with her. Still
the house is not the same, though she is the same.

It was these repeated illnesses of his sister, and the
loss of their old servant, that made them resolve to give
up housekeeping, and take lodgings next door ("Forty-
two inches nearer town," Lamb said), with an old couple a
Mr. and Mrs. Westwood, who undertook to board as well as
lodge them. "We have both had much illness this year,"
he wrote to a friend, "and feeling infirmities and fretful-
ness grow upon us, we have cast off the cares of housekeeping, sold off our goods, and commenced boarding and
lodging with a very comfortable old couple next door to
where you found us. We use a sort of common table.
Nevertheless, we have reserved a private one for an old

friend." In less than a week he was able to report the good effect of the change upon Mary. "She looks two and a half years younger for it. But we have had sore trials."

The next year opens with a letter to Wordsworth describing the new *ménage*, and containing a charming picture of the old couple who now were host and hostess as well as landlords.

Our providers are an honest pair, Dame Westwood and her husband; he, when the light of prosperity shined on them, a moderately thriving haberdasher within Bow Bells, retired since with something under a competence; writes himself parcel gentleman; hath borne parish offices; sings fine old sea-songs at threescore and ten; sighs only now and then when he thinks that he has a son on his hands about fifteen, whom he finds a difficulty in getting out into the world; and then checks a sigh with muttering, as I once heard him prettily, not meaning to be heard, "I have married my daughter, however;" takes the weather as it comes; outsides it to town in severest season; and o' winter nights tells old stories not tending to literature (how comfortable to author-rid folks!), and has *one anecdote*, upon which and about forty pounds a year he seems to have retired in green old age.

The letter gives encouraging news of his sister's health and spirits, but the loneliness and the want of occupation are pressing heavily, he says, upon himself. He yearns for London and the cheerful streets. "Let no native Londoner imagine that health and rest, innocent occupation, interchange of converse sweet, and recreative study, can make the country anything better than altogether odious and detestable." Later, in March, his thoughts are diverted from his own condition, by the illness of Miss Isola; and a proposal from John Murray to continue the *Specimens of the Old Dramatists* is declined, because in his anxiety for their young protégée he could think of nothing else. Miss Isola happily recovered. Lamb fetched her from Suffolk, where the illness had occurred, to Enfield, and it was on the journey home that the famous stage-coach incident occurred. " We travelled with one of those troublesome fellow-passengers in a stage coach that is called a well-informed man. For twenty miles we discoursed about the properties of steam, probabilities of carriage by ditto, till all my science, and more than all, was exhausted, and I was thinking of escaping my torment by getting up on the outside, when, getting into Bishop Stortford, my gentleman, spying some farming land, put an unlucky question to me : ' What sort of crop of turnips I thought we should have this year ? ' Emma's eyes turned to me, to know what in the world I could have to say ; and she burst into a violent fit of laughter, maugre her pale serious cheeks, when with the greatest gravity I replied that ' It depended, I believed, upon boiled legs of mutton.' "

There is little to record of incident or change in these last years of the life, now more and more lonely, of brother and sister. A small volume of occasional poetry, *Album Verses*—the amusements of the latter years of leisure— was produced by Mr. Moxon in 1830, but contains little to call for remark ; and another venture of Mr. Moxon's, *The Englishman's Magazine*, in the following year, drew from Lamb some prose contributions, under the heading of *Peter's Net*. In 1833, the Lambs made their last change of residence. Their furniture had been disposed of when they settled at Enfield, and they now entered on an arrangement similar to the last, of boarding and lodging with another married pair—younger, however, and more

M

active—a Mr. and Mrs. Walden, of Bay Cottage, in the
neighbouring parish of Edmonton. The reasons for the
change are of the old sad kind. A letter to Wordsworth, of May, 1833, tells the melancholy story:—
"Mary is ill again. Her illnesses encroach yearly. The
last was three months, followed by two of depression most
dreadful. I look back upon her earlier attacks with
longing. Nice little durations of six weeks or so, followed
by complete restoration, shocking as they were to me
then. In short, half her life is dead to me, and the other
half is made anxious with fears and lookings forward to
the next shock." Mary Lamb had been on former occasions of illness under the care of the Waldens, and the
increasing frequency of her attacks made this change
necessary in the interest of both brother and sister. It
secured for Mary the constant supervision of an attendant.

The same letter tells of an additional element of loneliness that was in store for them. Emma Isola was engaged
"with my perfect approval and entire concurrence" to
Mr. Moxon, the publisher, and the wedding was fixed.
Lamb writes of it with the old habitual unselfishness,
though it was to leave him without his "only walk-com-
panion, whose mirthful spirits were the 'youth of our
house.'" He turns, after his manner, to think of his com-
pensations. He is emancipated from Enfield, with attentive people and younger, and what is more, is three or
four miles nearer to his beloved town. Miss Isola was
married on the 30th of July, and it is pleasant to
know that though up to the very day of the wedding
Mary Lamb had been unable to interest herself in the
event, and was of course unable to be present at the
ceremony, she attributes her recovery from this attack to
the stimulus of the good news suddenly communicated.

There is a pathetic note of congratulation from her to the newly-married pair, in which she tells them of this with characteristic simplicity. The Waldens had with happy tact proposed Mr. and Mrs. Moxon's health, at their quiet meal. " It restored me from that moment," writes Mary Lamb, "as if by an electrical stroke, to the entire posses- sion of my senses. I never felt so calm and quiet after a similar illness as I do now. I feel as if all tears were wiped from my eyes, and all care from my heart." And Charles is able to add, in a postscript, how they are again happy in their old pursuits—cards, walks, and reading : "never was such a calm, or such a recovery."

In this year 1833, the later essays of Lamb contributed to the *London Magazine*, together with some shorter pieces from other periodicals, were published by Mr. Moxon, under the title of the *Last Essays of Elia*, and with this event the literary life of Lamb was destined to close. Nothing more, beyond an occasional copy of verses for a friend, came from his pen. Notwithstanding the increasing illness of his sister, he was able to enjoy some cheerful society, notably with a friend of recent date, Mr. Cary, the translator of *Dante*, with whom he dined periodically at the British Museum. Mr. John Forster, afterwards to be known widely as the author of the *Life of Goldsmith*, was another accession to his list of congenial friends. But these could not make compensation for the loss of the old. Lamb was not yet sixty years of age, but he was without those ties and relationships which more than all else we know bring "forward-looking thoughts." His life was lived chiefly in the past, and one by one "the old familiar faces" were passing away. In July, 1834, Coleridge died, after many months of suffering For the last eighteen years of his life he had resided

beneath Mr. Gilman's roof at Highgate, and Charles and
Mary Lamb were among the most welcome visitors at the
house : and now the friendship of fifty years was at an
end. All the little asperities of early rivalry ; all the
natural regrets at sight of a life so wasted—powers so vast
ending in performance so inadequate—a spirit so willing,
and a will so weak—were forgotten now. Lamb had never
spared the foibles of his old companion ; when Coleridge
had soared to his highest metaphysical flights he had
apologized for him—" Yes ! you know Coleridge is *so* full
of his fun ;"—he had described him as an " archangel, a
little damaged ;"—but the indescribable moral afflatus felt
through Coleridge's obscurest rhapsodies had been among
the best influences on Charles Lamb's life. A few
months later he tried to put his regrets and his obligations into words. " When I heard of the death of Coleridge, it was without grief. It seemed to me that he had
long been on the confines of the next world—that he had
a hunger for eternity. I grieved then that I could not
grieve ; but since, I feel how great a part he was of me.
His great and dear spirit haunts me. I cannot think a
thought, I cannot make a criticism on men or books,
without an ineffectual turning and reference to him. He
was the proof and touchstone of all my cogitations."
    The death of his friend was Charles Lamb's death-
blow. There had been two persons in the world for whom
he would have wished to live—Coleridge and his sister
Mary. The latter was now for the greater part of each
year worse than dead to him. The former was gone, and
the blank left him helplessly alone. In conversation with
friends he would suddenly exclaim, as if with surprise
that aught else in the world should interest him, " Coleridge is dead ! " And within five weeks of the day when

the touching tribute just cited was committed to paper, he
was called to join his friend. One day in the middle of
December, as he was taking his usual walk along the
London Road, his foot struck against a stone, and he
stumbled and fell, inflicting a slight wound on his face.
For some days the injury appeared trifling, and on
the 22nd of the month he writes a cheerful note to
the wife of his old friend George Dyer, concerning the
safety of a certain book belonging to Mr. Cary, which he
had left at her house. On the same day, however, symptoms of erysipelas supervened, and it soon became evident
that his general health was too feeble to resist the attack.
From the first appearance of the disease the failure of life
was so rapid that his intimate friends, Talfourd and Crabb
Robinson, did not reach his bed-side in time for him to
recognize them. The few words that escaped his lips
while his mind was still unclouded, conveyed to those who
watched him that he was undisturbed at the prospect of
death. His sister was, happily for herself, in no state to
feel or appreciate the blow that was falling. On the 27th of
December, murmuring in his last moments the names of
his dearest friends, he passed tranquilly out of life. " On
the following Saturday his remains were laid in a deep
grave in Edmonton churchyard, made in a spot which,
about a fortnight before, he had pointed out to his sister
on an afternoon wintry walk, as the place where he wished
to be buried."

There is a touching fitness in the circumstance that
Charles Lamb could not longer survive his earliest and
dearest friend—that, trying it for a little while, " he liked
it not—and died." It was a fitting comment on the circumstance, that that other great poet and thinker who next
to Coleridge shared Lamb's deepest pride and affection, as

he looked back a year afterwards on the gaps that death
had made in the ranks of those he loved, should have once
more linked their names in imperishable verse :—

> Nor has the rolling year twice measured
> From sign to sign its steadfast course,
> Since every mortal power of Coleridge
> Was frozen at its marvellous source.
>
> The rapt one of the godlike forehead,
> The heaven-eyed creature, sleeps in earth :
> And Lamb, the frolic and the gentle,
> Has vanished from his lonely hearth.

The friends of Lamb were not slow in giving expression
to their sorrow for his loss, and their admiration of his
character—Wordsworth and Landor in verse, Procter,
Moxon, Forster, and many others through various channels,
in prose. For the most part they had to deal in generali-
ties, for Mary Lamb still lived, and the full extent of her
brother's devotion and sacrifice could not yet be told.
But abundant testimony was forthcoming that (to borrow
Landor's words) he had left behind him that " worthier
thing than tears,"

> The love of friends, without a single foe.

Wordsworth, in a beautiful tribute to his friend, begun
with some view to an inscription for his grave, expressed
no more than the verdict of all who knew him well,
when he wrote,—

> Oh, he was good, if ever good man was.

And yet there must have been many of his old acquaintances who were startled at finding admiration for him
thus expressed. Those who were not aware of the conditions of his life, or knew him only on his ordinary
convivial side, regarded him, we are assured, as a flippant

talker, reckless indeed in speech, moody, and of uncertain temper. Few could know what Coleridge and Wordsworth and Southey knew so well, that with all his boastful renunciation of orthodoxy in belief, and his freedom of criticism on religious matters, he was one capable of feeling keenly both the sentiment and the principle of religious trust. There is ample evidence of this in those early letters written in the darkest hours of his life. And though the sentiment waned as a different class of associates gathered round him, and there were few at hand with whom to interchange his deeper thoughts, religion in him never died, but became a habit—a habit of enduring hardness, and cleaving to the steadfast performance of duty in face of the strongest allurements to the pleasanter and easier course. He set himself a task, one of the saddest and hardest that can be undertaken, to act as guardian and companion to one living always on the brink of insanity. For eight-and-thirty years he was faithful to this purpose, giving up everything for it, and never thinking that he had done enough, or could do enough, for his early friend, his " guardian angel."

It is noteworthy that those surface qualities of Charles Lamb by which so many were content to judge him, were just those which men are slow to connect with sterling goodness such as this. There was a certain Bohemianism in him, it must be allowed—a fondness for overmuch tobacco and gin-and-water, and for the company of those whom more particular people looked shy upon. He often fretted against the loss of time they caused him, but he was tolerant for the moment of what fed his sense of humour or fancy, and always of that which touched the " virtue of compassion " in him. He was free of speech, and not in the least afraid of shocking his company. And it seems a

natural inference that such traits betoken a hand-to-
mouth existence, a certain want of moral backbone,
irregularity in money matters, and the absence of any
settled purpose. Yet it was for the opposite of all this
that Lamb's life is so notable. He was well versed in
poverty—for some years in marked degree—but he seems
never to have exceeded his income, or to have been in
debt. In the days of his most straitened means he was
never so poor but that he had in reserve something to
help those poorer than himself. His letters show this
throughout; and as his own fortunes mended, his generosity
in giving becomes truly surprising. "He gave away
greatly," says his friend Mr. Procter, and goes on to relate
how on one occasion when he was in low spirits, and
Lamb imagined that it might proceed from pecuniary
causes, he said suddenly, "My dear boy, I have a quantity
of useless things—I have now in my desk a—a hundred
pounds—that I don't *know* what to do with. Take it."
In his more prosperous days he always had pensioners on
his bounty. For many years he allowed his old school-
mistress thirty pounds a year. To a friend of Southey's,
who was paralyzed, he paid ten pounds yearly ; and when
a subscription was raised for Godwin in his gravest difficulties, Lamb's contribution was the munificent one of
fifty pounds. His letters too prove that he could always
make the more difficult sacrifices of time and thought
when others were in need. For a young lady establishing
a school—for a poor fellow seeking an occasional clerkship
in the India House—for such as these he is continually
pleading and taking trouble. And before he knew that
the directors of the India House intended to provide for
his sister, in the event of her surviving him, on the
footing of a wife, he had managed to put by a sufficient

sum to place her beyond the reach of want. At his
death he left a sum of two thousand pounds, for his sister
during her life, with a reversion to the child of their
adoption, Emma Isola, then Mrs. Moxon.

Mary Lamb survived her brother nearly thirteen years,
dying at the advanced age of 82, on the 20th of May,
1847. After the death of Charles, her health rallied sufficiently for her to visit occasionally among their old
friends; but as years passed, her attacks became still
more frequent, and of longer duration, till her mind became
permanently enfeebled. After leaving Edmonton, she
lived chiefly in St. John's Wood, under the care of a
nurse. Her pension, together with the income from her
brother's savings, was amply sufficient for her few needs.

" She will live for ever in the memory of her friends,"
writes that true and faithful friend, Crabb Robinson,
" as one of the most amiable and admirable of women."
From this verdict there is no dissentient voice. With much
less from which to form a direct opinion than in her
brother's case, we seem to read her character almost
equally well. The tributes of her brother scattered
through essay and letter, her own few but very significant
letters, and her contributions to literature, show her
strong and healthy common sense, her true womanliness,
and her gift of keen and active sympathy. She shared
with Charles a love of Quaker-like colour and homeliness in dress. "She wore a neat cap," Mr. Procter tells
us, " of the fashion of her youth; an old-fashioned dress.
Her face was pale and somewhat square, but very placid,
with grey intelligent eyes. She was very mild in her
manners to strangers; and to her brother, gentle and
tender, always. She had often an upward look of peculiar
meaning when directed towards him, as though to give

him assurance that all was then well with her." This
unvarying manner, betokening mutual dependence and
interest, was the feature that most impressed all who
watched them together, her eyes often fixed on his
as on " some adoring disciple," and ever listening to help
his speech in some difficult word, and to anticipate the
coming need. He in turn was always on the watch to
detect any sign in her face of failing health or spirits, and
to divert the conversation, if occasion arose, from any
topic that might distress her or set up some dangerous
excitement. Among the strange and motley guests that
their hospitality brought around them, her own opinions
and habits remained, with little danger of being shaken.
" It has been the lot of my cousin," writes Lamb in the
essay *Mackery End*, " oftener perhaps than I could have
wished, to have had for her associates, and mine, free
thinkers, leaders and disciples of novel philosophies and
systems ; but she neither wrangles with, nor accepts their
opinions. That which was good and venerable to her
when she was a child, retains its authority over her mind
still. She never juggles or plays tricks with her understanding." It was this element of quietism in Mary
Lamb that made her so inestimable a companion for her
brother. She was strong where he was weak, and repose-
ful where he was so often ill at ease.

She was indeed fitted in all respects to be Charles
Lamb's life-long companion. She shared his worthiest
tastes, to the full. More catholic in her partialities than
he, she devoured modern books as well as ancient with
unfailing appetite, and had formed out of her reading
a pure and idiomatic English style, with just a touch, as
in everything else belonging to her, of an old-world formality. She possessed a distinct gift of humour, as her

portion of *Mrs. Leicester's School* amply shows.   The story
of the *Father's Wedding-day* has strokes of humour and
observation not unworthy of Goldsmith.   Landor used to
rave, with characteristic vehemence, about this little sketch,
and to declare that the incident of the child wishing,
when dressed in her new frock, that her poor " mamma
was alive, to see how fine she was on papa's wedding-day,"
was a masterpiece.   The story called *The Young Maho-
metan* has a special interest as containing yet one more
recollection of the old house at Blakesware.   The medal-
lions of the Twelve Cæsars, the Hogarth prints, and the
tapestry hangings, are all there, together with that picturesque incident, which Charles elsewhere has not overlooked, of the broken battledore and shuttlecock telling
of happy children's voices that had once echoed through
the lonely chambers.   It is certain that Charles and Mary,
ardently as they both clung in after years to London sights
and sounds, owed much both in genius and character to
having breathed the purer, calmer air of rural homesteads.

A common education, whether that of sweet garden
scenes, or the choice fancies and meditations of poet and
moralist—a sense of mutual need—a profound pity for
each other's frailties—of these was forged the bond that
held them, and years of suffering and self-denial had
made it ever more and more strong.   " That we had much
to struggle with, as we grew up together, we have reason
to be most thankful.   It strengthened and knit our com-
pact closer.   We could never have been what we have
been to each other, if we had always had the sufficiency
which you now complain of."   It is with these words of
divine philosophy that, when comparative ease had at
last been achieved, Charles Lamb could look back upon
the anxious past.

CHAPTER IX.

It remains to speak of those prose writings of Lamb, many of earlier date than the *Essays of Elia*, by which his quality as a critic must be determined. As early as 1811 he had published in Leigh Hunt's *Reflector* his essay on *The Genius and Character of Hogarth*. This was no subject taken up for the occasion. "His graphic representations," says Lamb, " are indeed books : they have the teeming, fruitful, suggestive meaning of *words* "—and no book was more familiar to him. A set of Hogarth's prints, including the *Harlot's* and *Rake's Progresses*, had been among the treasures of the old house at Blakesware ; and Lamb as a child had spelled through their grim and ghastly histories again and again, till he came to know every figure and incident in them by heart. And now the cavalier tone in which certain leaders of the classical and historical schools of painting were wont to dismiss Hogarth as of slight value in point of art, made him keen to vindicate his old favourite. He has scant patience with those who noted defective drawing or " knowledge of the figure," in the artist. He is intolerant altogether of technical criticism. The essay is devoted to showing how true a moralist the painter is, and how false the view which would regard him chiefly as a humorist. He is a great satirist—a Juve-

nal or a Persius. Moreover, he is a combination of satirist
and dramatist. Hogarth had claimed for his pictures that
they should be judged as successive scenes in a play, and
Lamb takes him at his word. He is carried away by admiration for the tragic power displayed. He is in ecstasies
over the print of *Gin Lane*, certainly one of the poorest of
Hogarth's pictures as a composition, losing its due effect by
overcrowding of incident, and made grotesque through
sheer exaggeration. Yet, what stirs the critic's heart is
"the pity of it," and he is in no humour to admit other
considerations. He calls it "a sublime print." "Every part
is full of strange images of death ; it is perfectly amazing
and astounding to look at ;" and so forth. It is noticeable
that Lamb does not write with the pictures before him,
and trusts to a memory not quite trustworthy. For example, to prove that Hogarth is not merely repulsive, that
there is always a sweet humanity in reserve as a foil for
the horrors he deals with—something to " keep the general
air from tainting," he says : " Take the mild, supplicating
posture of patient poverty, in the poor woman that is per-
suading the pawnbroker to accept her clothes in pledge in
the plate of *Gin Lane*." There is really no such incident
in the picture. There is a woman offering in pawn her
kettle and fire-irons ; but, taken in combination with all
the other incidents of the scene, she is certainly pledging
them to buy gin. Here, as elsewhere, Lamb damages his
case by over-statement, partly through love of surprises,
partly because he willingly discovered in poem or picture
what he wished to find there. He sees more of humanity
and sweetness in what affects him than is actually present.
He *reads* something of himself into the composition he is
reviewing. He is on safer ground when he dwells on the
genuine power, the pity and the terror, in that last scene but

one of *The Marriage-à-la-Mode ;* and on the gentleness of
the wife's countenance, poetizing the whole scene, in the
print of *The Distressed Poet.* And he is doing a service
to art of larger scope than fixing the respective ranks of
Hogarth and Poussin, in these noble concluding lines :—

I say not that all the ridiculous subjects of Hogarth have
necessarily something in them to make us like them ; some are
indifferent to us, some in their natures repulsive, and only made
interesting by the wonderful skill and truth to nature in the
painter ; but I contend that there is in most of them that sprink-
ling of the better nature which, like holy water, chases away
and disperses the contagion of the bad. They have this in them
besides, that they bring us acquainted with the every-day human
face ; they give us skill to detect those gradations of sense and
virtue (which escape the careless or fastidious observer) in the
countenances of the world about us ; and prevent that disgust
at common life, that *tædium quotidianarum formarum,* which
an unrestricted passion for ideal forms and beauties is in danger
of producing.

His judgments of pictures are, as might be expected, those
of a man of letters, not of a painter. It is the *story* in the
picture that impresses him, and the technical qualities leave
him unmoved. A curious instance of this is afforded in his
essay on *The Barrenness of the Imaginative Faculty in the
Productions of Modern Art.* After complaining that, with
the exception of Hogarth, no artist within the last fifty
years had treated a story *imaginatively*—" upon whom his
subject has so acted that it has seemed to direct *him,* not
to be arranged by him "—he breaks out into a fine rhap-
sody on the famous *Bacchus and Ariadne* of Titian in the
National Gallery. But it is not as a masterpiece of colour
and drawing that it excites his admiration. The qualities
of the poet, not those of the painter, are what he discovers

in it. It is the "imaginative faculty" which he detects, as shown in the power of uniting the past and the present. "Precipitous, with his reeling satyr-rout around him, re-peopling and re-illuming suddenly the waste places, drunk with a new fury beyond the grape, Bacchus, born of fire, fire-like flings himself at the Cretan : " this is the *present*. Ariadne, "unconscious of Bacchus, or but idly casting her eyes as upon some unconcerning pageant, her soul undistracted from Theseus"—Ariadne, "pacing the solitary shore in as much heart-silence, and in almost the same local solitude, with which she awoke at day-break to catch the forlorn last glances of the sail that bore away the Athenian ; " this is the *past*. But it is in the situation itself, not in Titian's treatment of it, that Lamb has found the antithesis that so delights him. He is in fact the poet, taking the subject out of the painter's hands, and treating it afresh. Lamb obtains an easy victory for the ancients over the moderns, by choosing as his foil for Titian and Raffaelle the treatment of sacred subjects by Martin, the painter of *Belshazzar's Feast* and *The Plains of Heaven*. And it is significant of a certain inability in Lamb to do full justice to his contemporaries, that in noting the barrenness of the fifty years in question in the matter of art, he has no exception to make but Hogarth. He might have had a word to say for Turner and Wilkie.

The essay on *The Artificial Comedy of the Last Century* has received more attention than its importance at all warrants, from the circumstance that Macaulay set to work seriously to demolish its reasoning, in reviewing Leigh Hunt's edition of the Restoration Dramatists. Lamb's essay was originally part of a larger essay upon the old actors, in which he was led to speak of the comedies of

Congreve and Wycherley, and the reasons why they no longer held the stage. His line of defence is well known. He protests that the world in which their characters move is so wholly artificial—a conventional world, quite apart from that of real life—that it is beside the mark to judge them by any moral standard. "They are a world of themselves almost as much as fairy-land." The apology is really (as Hartley Coleridge acutely points out) for those who, like himself, could enjoy the wit of these writers, without finding their actual judgment of moral questions at all influenced by it. It must be admitted that Lamb does not convince us of the sincerity of his reasoning, and probably he did not convince himself. He loved paradox ; and he loved, moreover, to find some soul of goodness in things evil. As Hartley Coleridge adds, it was his way always to take hold of things " by the better handle."

The same love of paradox is manifest in the essay on *Shakespeare's Tragedies*, "considered with reference to their fitness for stage representation." If there are any positions which we should *not* expect to find Lamb disputing, they are the acting qualities of Shakespeare's plays, and the intellectual side of the actor's art. Yet these are what he devotes this paper to impugning. He had been much disgusted by the fulsome flattery contained in the epitaph on Garrick in Westminster Abbey. In this bombastic effusion, this "farrago of false thoughts and nonsense," as Lamb calls it, Garrick is put on a level with Shakespeare :—

> And till Eternity with power sublime
> Shall mark the mortal hour of hoary Time,
> Shakespeare and Garrick like twin-stars shall shine,
> And earth irradiate with a beam divine.

Why is it, asks Lamb, that "from the days of the

actor here celebrated to our own, it should have been the
fashion to compliment every performer in his turn, that
has had the luck to please the town in any of the great
characters of Shakespeare, with the notion of possessing *a
mind congenial with the poet's:* how people should come
thus unaccountably to confound the power of originating
poetical images and conceptions with the faculty of being
able to read or recite the same when put into words ? "
And he goes on, in the same strain of contempt, to speak
of the "low tricks upon the eye and ear," which the
player can so easily compass, as contrasted with the " absolute mastery over the heart and soul of man, which a
great dramatic poet possesses."   No one knew better than
Lamb, that the resources of the actor's art are not fairly
or adequately stated in such language as this.   He had
himself the keenest relish for good acting, and no one
has described and criticised it more finely.   Witness his
description of his favourite Munden, in the part of the
Greenwich Pensioner, Old Dosey, and of Bensley's conception of the character of Malvolio.   Or, again, take the
exquisite passage in which he recalls Mrs. Jordan's performance of Viola : "There is no giving an account how
she delivered the disguised story of her love for Orsino.
It was no set speech, that she had foreseen, so as to weave
it into a harmonious period, line necessarily following line
to make up the music—yet I have heard it so spoken, or
rather *read,* not without its grace and beauty ; but when
she had declared her sister's history to be a "blank," and
that she "never told her love," there was a pause, as if
the story had ended—and then the image of the "worm
in the bud " came up as a new suggestion—and the
heightened image of "Patience " still followed after that,
as by some growing (and not mechanical) process, thought

N

springing up after thought, I would almost say, as they
were watered by her tears." We are quite sure that
the writer of these eloquent words did not seriously
regard the art of acting as a mere succession of tricks
"upon the eye and ear." He was for the moment
prejudiced against the great actor—whom, by the way, he
had never seen, Garrick having left the stage in 1776—by
the injudicious language of his flatterers. But if we make
due allowance for his outburst of spleen, we shall find
much that is admirably true mixed up with it. Critics
have often, for instance, insisted upon what is gained by
seeing a drama acted, as distinguished from reading it,
and Lamb here devotes himself to showing how far it is
from being all gain. "It is difficult for a frequent play-
goer to disembarrass the idea of Hamlet from the person
and voice of Mr. Kemble. We speak of Lady Macbeth,
while we are in reality thinking of Mrs. Siddons." We
get distinctness, says Lamb, from seeing a character thus
embodied, but "dearly do we pay" for this sense of
distinctness.

This line of criticism leads up to the crowning paradox
of this essay, that the plays of Shakespeare "are less
calculated for performance on a stage than those of almost
any other dramatist whatever." Here again it may be
said that no one knew better than Lamb that in a
most important sense these words are the very reverse of
truth. There is no quality in which Shakespeare's greatness as a dramatist is more conspicuous than his knowledge of what is effective in stage representation. But
Lamb chose to mean something very different from this.
He was thinking of certain other qualities in the poet
which are incommunicable by the medium of acting, and
on these he proceeds to dwell, discussing for that purpose

the traditional stage rendering of Hamlet and other characters. He points out how the stage Hamlet almost always overdoes his scorn for Polonius, and his brutality to Ophelia, and asks the reason of this. It does not seem to occur to him that this is simply *bad* acting, and that it is not at all a necessary incident of the art that Hamlet's feelings should be thus represented. He seems to be confounding the limitations of the particular actor with those of his art. Indeed it is clear that many of the positions maintained in this paper are simply convenient opportunities for enlarging upon some character or conception of the great dramatist.

Lamb had a juster complaint against Garrick than that supplied by the words of a foolish epitaph. He boldly expresses a doubt whether the actor was capable of any real admiration for Shakespeare. Would any true lover of his plays, he asks, have "admitted into his matchless scenes such ribald trash" as Tate and Cibber and the rest had foisted into the acting versions of the dramas? Much of the scorn and indignation expressed by Lamb in this paper, becomes intelligible when we recall in what garbled shapes the dramatist was presented. Garrick himself had taken a prominent share in these alterations of the text. It was he who completely changed the last act of *Hamlet,* and turned the *Winter's Tale* into a piece of Arcadian insipidity. But the greatest outrage of all, in Lamb's view, would be Tate's version of Lear—in a modified edition of which Garrick himself had performed. In this version—which the editor of Bell's acting edition (1774) calls a "judicious blending" of Shakespeare and Tate—the character of the Fool is altogether omitted ; Cordelia survives, and marries Edgar ; and Lear, Kent, and Gloster announce their intention of retiring into

N 2

private life, to watch the happiness of the young couple,
Lear himself bringing down the curtain with these
amazing lines :—

> Thou, Kent, and I, retired from noise and strife,
> Will calmly pass our short reserves of time
> In cool reflections on our fortunes past,
> Cheered with relation of the prosperous reign
> Of this celestial pair ; thus our remains
> Shall in an even course of thoughts be past,
> Enjoy the present hour, nor fear the last.

This was the stuff which in Lamb's day the actors and
their audience were content to accept as the work of the
Master-hand.   It may well account for a tone of bitterness,
and even of exaggeration, that pervades the essay.   It is
some compensation that it drew from Lamb his noble vindication of Shakespeare's original.   The passage is well
known, but I cannot deny myself the pleasure of quoting
it once again :—

The Lear of Shakespeare cannot be acted.   The contemptible
machinery by which they mimic the storm which he goes out
in, is not more inadequate to represent the horrors of the real
elements, than any actor can be to represent Lear ; they might
more easily propose to personate the Satan of Milton upon a
stage, or one of Michael Angelo's terrible figures.   The greatness of Lear is not in corporal dimension, but in intellectual ;
the explosions of his passion are terrible as a volcano ; they are
storms turning up and disclosing to the bottom that sea, his
mind, with all its vast riches.   It is his mind which is laid bare.
This case of flesh and blood seems too insignificant to be thought
on : even as he himself neglects it.   On the stage we see nothing
but corporal infirmities and weakness, the impotence of rage :
while we read it, we see not Lear, but we *are* Lear, we are in
his mind, we are sustained by a grandeur which baffles the
malice of daughters and storms ; in the aberrations of his
reason we discover a mighty irregular power of reasoning, im-

methodized from the ordinary purposes of life, but exerting its powers, as the wind blows where it listeth, at will upon the corruptions and abuses of mankind. What have looks or tones to do with that sublime identification of his age with that of the *heavens themselves*, when in his reproaches to them for conniving at the injustice of his children, he reminds them that "they themselves are old?" What gestures shall we appropriate to this? What has the voice or the eye to do with such things? But the play is beyond all art, as the tamperings with it show: it is too hard and stony; it must have love-scenes, and a happy ending. It is not enough that Cordelia is a daughter; she must shine as a lover too. Tate has put his hook in the nostrils of this Leviathan, for Garrick and his followers, the showmen of the scene, to draw the mighty beast about more easily. A happy ending!—as if the living martyrdom that Lear had gone through, the flaying of his feelings alive, did not make a fair dismissal from the stage of life the only decorous thing for him. If he is to live and be happy after, if he could sustain this world's burden after, why all this pudder and preparation—why torment us with all this unnecessary sympathy? as if the childish pleasure of getting his gilt robes and sceptre again could tempt him to act over again his misused station—as if, at his years, and with his experience, anything was left but to die.

No passage in Lamb's writings is better fitted than this to illustrate his peculiar power as a commentator. It as little suggests Hazlitt or Coleridge, as it does Schlegel or Gervinus. It is more remote still—it need hardly be added—from the fantastic tricks of a later day, which are doing all they can to make Shakespearian criticism hideous. Lamb's emphatic vindication of the course of events in Shakespeare's tragedy of course implies a criticism and a commendation of the dramatist. But no one feels that he is either patronizing, or judging, Shakespeare. He takes Lear, as it were, out of the hands of literature, and regards him as a human being placed in the world

where all men have to suffer and be tempted. We forget
that he is a character in a play, or even in history.
Lamb's criticism is a commentary on life, and no truer
homage could be paid to the dramatist than that he
should be allowed for the time to pass out of our
thoughts.

Thoroughly characteristic of Lamb is the admirable
paper on *The Sanity of True Genius,* suggested by
Dryden's famous line as to "great wit" being nearly
allied to madness. It aims to disprove this, and to show
that, on the contrary, the greatest wits "will ever be
found to be the sanest writers." He illustrates this by
the use that Shakespeare and others make of the supernatural persons and situations in their writings. "Cali-
ban, the Witches, are as true to the laws of their own
nature (ours with a difference) as Othello, Hamlet, and
Macbeth. Herein the great and the little wits are differ-
enced : that if the latter wander ever so little from nature
or actual existence, they lose themselves and their
readers." And with a marvellous semblance of paradox,
which yet is felt to be profoundly true, he proceeds to declare that in Spenser's Episode of the "Cave of Mammon,"
where the Money-God, and his daughter Ambition and
Pilate washing his hands—the most discordant persons
and situations—are introduced, the controlling power of
the poet's sanity makes the whole more actually consistent, than the characters and situations of every-day life
in the latest novel from the Minerva Press. It is a proof,
he says, "of that hidden sanity which still guides the
poet in his wildest seeming aberrations." No detached
sentences can, however, convey an idea of this splendid
argument. Nothing that Lamb has written proves more
decisively how large a part the higher imagination plays

in true criticism; nothing better illustrates the truth of
Butler's claim, that

> The poet must be tried by his peers,
> And not by pedants and philosophers.

That Lamb was a poet is at the root of his greatness
as a critic; and his own judgments of poetry show the
same sanity to which he points in his poetical brethren.
He is never so impulsive or discursive that he fails to
show how unerring is his judgment on all points connected with the poet's art.   There had been those before
Lamb, for example, who had quoted and called attention to
the poetry of George Wither; but no one had thought of
noticing that his metre was also that of Ambrose Philips,
and that Pope and his friends had only proved their own
defective ear by seeking to make it ridiculous. "To the
measure in which these lines are written, the wits of
Queen Anne's days contemptuously gave the name of
Namby-Pamby, in ridicule of Ambrose Philips, who has
used it in some instances, as in the lines on Cuzzoni, to
my feeling at least very deliciously; but Wither, whose
darling measure it seems to have been, may show that in
skilful hands it is capable of expressing the subtlest
movement of passion.   So true it is, what Drayton seems
to have felt, that it is the poet who modifies the metre,
not the metre the poet."

It was in the margin of a copy of Wither's poems that
this exquisite comment was originally made; and in such
a casual way did much of Lamb's finest criticism come
into being.   All through his life, in letter and essay,
he was making remarks of this kind, throwing them out
by the way, never thinking that they would be hereafter
treasured up as the most luminous and penetrative judg-

ments of the century. And it may well be asked why, with such a range of sympathy, from Marlowe to Ambrose Philips, from Sir T. Browne to Sir William Temple, he was so limited, so one-sided in his estimate of the literature of his own age? It is true that he was among the first in England to appreciate Burns and Wordsworth. But to Scott, Byron, and Shelley he entertained a feeling almost of aversion. He was glad (as we gather from the Essay on *The Sanity of True Genius*) that "a happier genius" had arisen to expel the "innutritious phantoms" of the Minerva Press; but the success of the Waverley Novels seems to have caused him amusement rather than any other feeling. About Byron, he wrote to Joseph Cottle, " I have a thorough aversion to his character, and a very moderate admiration of his genius : he is great in so little a way. To be a poet is to be the man, not a petty portion of occasional low passion worked up in a permanent form of humanity." Shelley's poetry, he told Barton he did not understand, and that it was "thin sown with profit or delight." When he read Goethe's *Faust* (of course in an English version), he at once pronounced it inferior to Marlowe's in the chief *motive* of the plot, and was evidently content to let criticism end there. Something of this may be ascribed to a jealousy in Lamb —a strange and needless jealousy for his own loved writers of the sixteenth and seventeenth centuries, and a fear lest the new comers should usurp some of the praise and renown that he claimed for them ; something, also, to a perverseness in him which made him like to be in opposition to the current opinion, whatever it might be. He was often unwilling, rather than unable, to discuss the claims of a new candidate for public favour. He lived mainly in communion with an older literature. It was to

him inexhaustible in amount and in excellence, and he
was impatient of what sought to divert his attention from
it.   It was literally true of him that " when a new book
came out—he read an old one."

But even of the old ones, the classics of our literature,
it was not easy to say what his opinion in any case would
be.   For instance, he was a great admirer of Smollett, and
was with great difficulty brought to admit the superiority
of Fielding.   And in the work of a greater humorist than
Smollett, in the Picaresque school—*Gil Blas*—he would
not acknowledge any merit at all.   The truth is that for
Lamb to enjoy a work of humour, it must embody a
strong human interest, or at least have a pulse of humanity
throbbing through it.   Humour, without pity or tenderness, only repelled him.   It was another phase of the
same quality in him that—as we have seen in his estimate
of Byron—where he was not drawn to the *man*, he was
almost disabled from admiring, or even understanding,
the man's work.   Had he ever come face to face with the
author for a single evening, the result might have been
quite different.

There is no difficulty, therefore, in detecting the limitations of Lamb as a critic.   In a most remarkable degree
he had the defects of his qualities.   Where his heart was,
there his judgment was sound.   Where he actively dis-
liked, or was passively indifferent, his critical powers
remained dormant.   He was too fond of paradox, too
much at the mercy of his emotions or the mood of the
hour, to be a safe guide always.   But where no disturbing
forces interfered, he exercised a faculty almost unique in
the history of criticism.   When Southey heard of his
Specimens of the English Dramatic Poets, he wrote to
Coleridge : " If co-operative labour were as practicable as

it is desirable, what a history of English literature might he and you and I set forth!" Such an enterprise would be, as Southey saw, all but impossible; but if the spiritual insight of Coleridge, and the unwearied industry and sober common-sense of Southey, could be combined with the special genius of Charles Lamb, something like the ideal commentary on English literature might be the result.

As it is, Lamb's contribution to that end is of the rarest value. If it is too much to say that he singly revived the sixteenth and seventeenth centuries, it is because we see clearly that that revival was coming, and would have come even without his help. But he did more than recall attention to certain forgotten writers. He flashed a light from himself upon them, not only heightening every charm and deepening every truth, but making even their eccentricities beautiful and lovable. And in doing this he has linked his name for ever with theirs. When we think of "the sweetest names, and which carry a perfume in the mention,—Kit Marlowe, Drayton, Drummond of Hawthornden, and Cowley"—then the thought of Charles Lamb will never be far off. His name, too, has a perfume in the mention. "There are some reputations," wrote Southey to Caroline Bowles, "which will not keep, but Lamb's is not of that kind. His memory will retain its fragrance as long as the best spice that ever was expended upon one of the Pharaohs."

THE END.

LONDON :
PRINTED BY GILBERT AND RIVINGTON, LIMITED,
ST. JOHN'S SQUARE.